Google Tools for Teaching & Learning

Table of Contents

Google Tools for Teaching and Learning

Google Tools
For Teaching and Learning

Tammy Worcester

VISIONS™
TECHNOLOGY IN EDUCATION
PUBLISHER OF QUALITY EDUCATIONAL PRODUCTS

Production Coordinator
John Crowder

Copy Editor
David Hoerger

Cover Design
Tim Yost

Visions Technology
P.O. Box 70479
Eugene, OR 97401

Phone: 541.349.0905
Fax: 541.349.0944
Email: info@teamvistech.com
Web site: www.toolsforteachers.com

ISBN: 978-1-58912-875-0

Google's Search Tools

Of course you can use Google as a search tool. But did you know that you could use it for much more than that? In this section, you'll learn all sorts of tips and tricks for searching!

Google's Search Tools

Google Search Tricks
In the Google search window, try the following:

- **Calculator**
  Type a calculation and press enter.
  You'll see the answer in the results window.
  Use the asterisks (shift + 8) for the multiplication symbol and the slash (under the question mark) for the division symbol.

  25 + 35 * 3 / 4 – 2
  1535 – 276
  14 * 3 - 6

- **Conversion Tool**
  Type something similar to one of the following and press enter:
  Be sure to use the word "in."

  1 mile in feet
  1 cup in tablespoons
  100 dollars in Euros
  180 c in f

- **Dictionary**
  Type "Define:" and then the word you want defined:

  define: pragmatic
  define: congruent
  define: socialism

- **Weather**
  Type the word "weather" and then the city (or city and state) and then press return to see the weather conditions for the next 5 days:

  weather Wichita
  weather London
  weather Portland, OR

- **Flight Search**

  Enter the airline, or the airline , and your flight number and press return to see the flight status:

  American 5324
  AA 5324
  United 786
  UA 786

- **Movie Search**

  Enter "movie:" and your zip code and press return. This will return a list of theaters, movies, times, and even reviews!

  movie: 67226
  movie: 90210

Google Search Tips

These tips will help to refine your Google search:

- Use quotation marks to search for a phrase:

  "cooperative learning"

- Restrict the search by using the minus sign:

  If you want information about the ship, try: titanic –movie

- Try a wildcard search using the asterisk:

  Don't enter: What's the capital of Kansas?
  Enter: The capital of Kansas is *

Using Google to Find PowerPoint Presentations

You can use the features in the Advanced Google Search area to find PowerPoint presentations that are already created!

Searching for PowerPoint Presentations

1. Go to: www.google.com

2. Click the "Advanced Search" link at the right of the search window.

3. In the Advanced Search area:
   a. Enter the desired search terms. (These may be key words of topics you will be teaching soon.)

   b. Choose the File Type – Microsoft PowerPoint.

   c. Click the "Advanced Search" button.

   d. This will return a list of PowerPoint files.
   Note – In the example below, a search for PowerPoint files with the words "simple machines" returned 21,200 results.

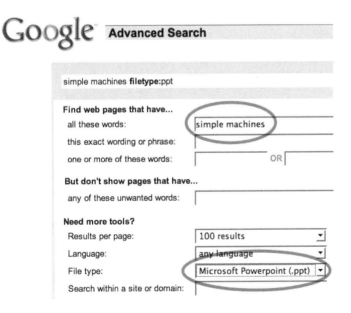

Opening and Viewing PowerPoint Presentations

On the results page, you'll see a title and a description for each PowerPoint file.

1. To view the file in your browser:
    Click the "View as HTML" link.

2. To open the file in PowerPoint:
    a. Click the title and choose to save the file.
        or
        Right-click (Win) or Control-click (Mac) the title and choose "save target as" or "save link as" (or something similar).

    b. Double-click the saved file and it will open in PowerPoint.

        Note – Once the file is open in PowerPoint, you can edit and customize it to fit your needs! Just be sure to give credit to the original author!

Finding PowerPoint Games

Many teachers have created games using PowerPoint. You can find those by using Google's Advanced Search options:

1. Add the word "jeopardy" or "millionaire" to your key word.

2. Choose the File Type, Microsoft PowerPoint.

3. Click the "Advanced Search" button. Then follow the instructions above to open and use the game. Be sure to view the file as a "Slide Show" to play the game!

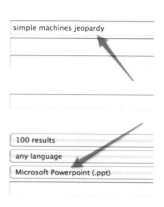

Creating a Custom Google Search Engine

Want to limit the sites your students can search? You can create your own Google search engine that will search only the websites that you choose.

Example

The search engine pictured above is designed to search only these sites: kids.yahoo.com; www.awesomelibrary.com; www.iknowthat.com; and www.wikipedia.org.

You can try it at: http://tinyurl.com/twcustomsearch

Creating the Custom Search Engine

1. Go to: http://www.google.com/coop/cse/

2. Sign in using your Google account information. (If you don't have a Google account, see page 133.)

3. Click the "Create a Custom Search Engine" button.

4. Follow the on-screen prompts and fill out the necessary information to create your own search engine.

Editing the Custom Search Engine

1. Go to: http://www.google.com/coop/cse/

2. Click the "manage your existing search engines" link.

3. Choose the "control panel" option.

4. In the control panel, click the links at the top to edit different categories.

Sharing Your Custom Search Engine
You can share your search engine with others in two ways:

a. Share the address (URL):
    Go to the homepage of your custom search engine and
    locate the address of the page. (See page 139 for tips for
    sharing a long URL.)

> http://www.google.com/coop/cse?cx=002915982925413064353:pjplbeppgt4 ▼

b. Use the provided code to embed a custom search box
    widget into your blog, webpage, or a wiki. (To see how
    to use embed code in a blog, see page 48.)

Control panel: Tammy Worcester's Search Engine
Basics | Sites | Indexing | Refinements | Look and feel | Code | Collabo

Google Image Search
Want to show students who Albert Einstein is or what a
kumquat looks like? Try using Google's Image Search.

Using Google Image Search

1. Go to: www.google.com

2. Click the "Images" link.

3. Enter the desired keyword(s).

4. Click the "Search Images" button.
    When the search is complete you will see a page
    (or pages) of thumbnail pictures.

5. In the results page, you can filter the image type.
    a. Locate the "Any Content" pull-down menu.
    b. Click the arrow and choose the type of image
        you want: faces; clip art; line drawings; etc.

6. To view a larger image:
    a. Click the desired thumbnail image.
        This will open a new page.
    b. At the top of the page, click the link that says,
        "See full size image."

Google Book Search

Google's book search allows you to search the contents of a book or magazine and then helps you purchase it or find it in a local library!

Using Google's Book Search

1. Go to: books.google.com

2. Enter the desired keywords. *(Maybe something school-related like raising test scores or project-based learning – or something fun like herb gardening.)*

3. Click the "Search Books" button.

4. Browse the list of books and click one that looks interesting.

   Note – some books will allow you to look through the pages and search within the book, others will not.

5. At the right, you'll see options for buying the book or borrowing the book.
   a. Click one of the vendors to purchase the book online and have it shipped to you.

   b. Click the "find in a library" link to see the libraries near you that have the book available for checkout.

Buy this book
Amazon.com
Barnes&Noble.com
Books-A-Million
BookSense.com
Google Product Search

Borrow this book
Find this book in a library

Creating Your Own Book Search "Library"

You and/or your students* can keep track of, review, and share your favorite books using the "My Library" feature of Google's Book Search.

As a teacher, you could create a library of suggested books for your students. A student could keep track of (and review) books he/she has read during the school year.

* Students will need individual Google accounts to create their own libraries. If you use a single generic student login, they can create a collaborative library.

Books in my library

Creating Your Library

1. Go to: books.google.com

2. Click the "My library" link in the upper-right corner.

3. Sign in to your Google Account.

4. Search for a book title and/or author.

5. When you find the desired book, click the "Add to my library" link.

Viewing/Editing Your Library

1. Click the "My library" link in the upper-right corner.

2. Toggle between the list view and the cover view by clicking the links in the upper-right corner.

3. In the list view, you can:
   - Add notes.
   - Add labels.
   - Write a review.
   - Delete the book from your library.

Sharing Your Library

1. You can send others to your library using the URL in the location window of your browser.

2. See page 139 for Tips for Sharing a Long URL.

Google News
Use Google's News search option to search for news
articles, headlines, and current events!

Browsing for News

1. Go to: news.google.com or click the "News"
    link at the top of: www.google.com

2. Click the category labels at the left to browse the
    current news headlines for world, U.S.,
    Business, etc.

Searching for News

1. Go to: news.google.com or click the "News"
    link at the top of: www.google.com

2. Enter the desired keyword(s) in the search
    window.

3. Click the "Search News" button.

4. On the results page:
    a. Click the links at the top to sort by relevance
        or date.

    b. Click the links at the left to narrow results to
        a certain time period.

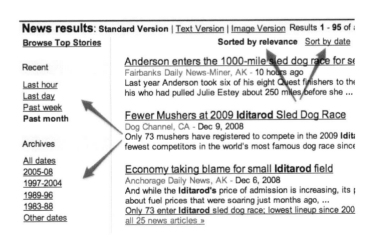

Other Google Searches

There are more specialized Google searches that can make it easy to find the information you want.

1. Go to: www.google.com

2. Click the links at the top of the page.

   or

3. Click the "more" link and pull down to see additional search tools.

iGoogle & Google Alerts

Imagine this scenario. Each morning you sit down at your computer and do the following: you go to your email site to check for new messages; you visit additional Web pages to check your horoscope, to see what the stock market is doing, and to read the latest news headlines; a glance at a weather site helps you decide what to wear for the day; another page teaches you a new vocabulary word or provides an inspiration quote for the day; if you have time, you go to yet another page and play a quick game of online Sudoku.

In that scenario, you have visited at least 5 or 6 different Web pages – and maybe even more!

Wouldn't it be nice to have a one-stop website with all of the information and tools you want right at your fingertips. Well, you're in luck – that's exactly what iGoogle provides for you!

Note – A Google Account is required for iGoogle.

Google Alerts

Instead of continuously searching for the latest news and newest websites, you can use Google alerts to bring the information right to your email inbox!

*You do **not** need a Google account to create or cancel Google Alerts.*

iGoogle

Getting started

1. Go to: www.google.com

2. If you aren't already logged in, click the "Sign In" link in the upper-right corner.

3. Click the "iGoogle" link in the upper-right corner. (Note - You can easily toggle back and forth between the classic view and the iGoogle view.)

Exploring the screen

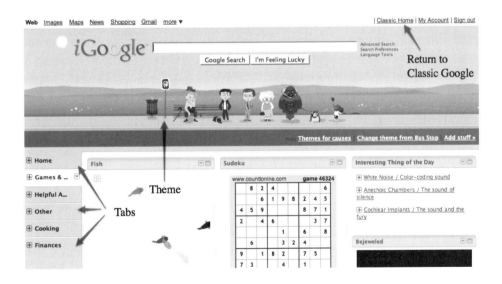

Setting up iGoogle
Google will help you to set up your pages, and/or you can customize them manually.

Here are some options:

- **Tabs**
  You can organize your information within tabs that show at the left side of the screen. To add/edit tabs, click the triangle to access the drop-down menu.

- **Themes**
  Each tab can have its own theme displayed at the top of the screen. Click one of the links as shown below to select or change the theme.

  Some themes will ask for your zip code and then will change to fit the current conditions for your area. The "bus stop" theme, shown here, will change depending on the weather. The screen shot above was taken on a cloudy day.

- **Gadgets** (stuff)
  Now it is time to fill your tabs with stuff! Move to the desired tab first, then click the "Add stuff" link.

1. Browse the gadgets by clicking the categories at the left, or use the search window at the upper-right to find the desired gadgets.

2. Click the "Add it now" button for each gadget you want on your page (for the Tab you selected). Then click the "Back to iGoogle home" link.

3. You can drag and drop the gadgets to new locations on the page (just click and drag the top), and you can customize and edit them by clicking the triangle in the upper-right corner.

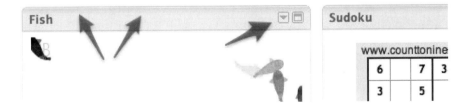

Google Alerts

Use Google alerts to bring the information right to your email inbox!

*You do **not** need a Google account to create or cancel Google Alerts.*

Creating a Google Alert

1. Go to: www.google.com/alerts

2. Enter the desired topic or keyword(s).

3. Choose the desired type:
   Note – "Comprehensive" includes all categories.
   a. News
   b. Blogs
   c. Web
   d. Comprehensive
   e. Video
   f. Groups

4. Decide how often you want the alerts emailed to you:
   a. As is happens
   b. Once a day
   c. Once a week

5. Enter your email address.

6. Click the "Create Alert" button.

7. Check your email for a message from Google.

8. Click the link in the email message to verify the alert.

Receiving/Removing Alerts

You will receive an email message whenever there's new information about your topic!

At the bottom of the email message, you'll find an option that will allow you to "Remove" the alert.

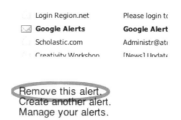

Google Maps

Google Maps will allow you to locate an address, find directions, and more!

*Note – This chapter of the book is divided into two sections: Google Maps Basics, and Google Maps Advanced. The activities in the "basic" section do not require a Google Account; the activities in the "advanced" section **do** require a Google Account.*

Google Maps

Google Maps Basics

Locating an Address

1. Go to: maps.google.com
   or
   Go to www.google.com and click the "Maps" link at
   the upper-left.

2. Enter an address in the search window.

3. Click the "Search Maps" button.

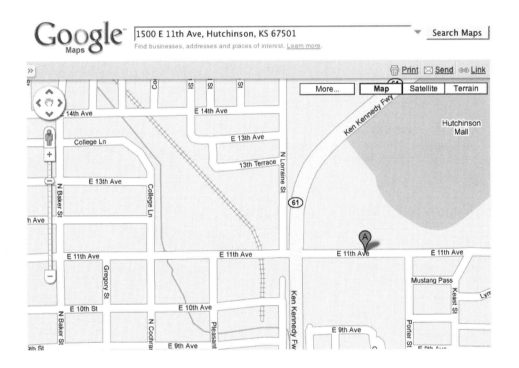

Exploring the Map

Refer to the image at the right to learn about some of the map features.

1. Click to expand the map. Click again to make the map smaller.

2. Click the arrows on this tool to move the map up, down, left, or right.

3. Look at a street view (if available). Click the "x" to close the street view.

4. Use the + and – buttons to zoom in and out.

5. Click this marker for more information about the location.

6. View different types of maps by clicking "Map," "Satellite," or "Terrain."

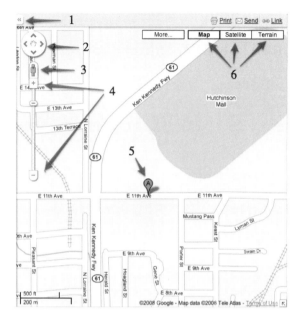

Finding Nearby Businesses

1. Click the placemark icon to open the address window.

2. Click the "Search nearby" link.

3. In the provided window, enter something like pizza, mall, Walgreens, spa, movie theater, or hotel.

4. Click the "Search" button.

5. The resulting map will show:
   a. Placemarks for each location. Click a placemark to get directions.
   b. The left side of the map will show a list of related locations, starting with the one that is closest.

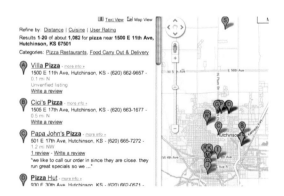

Getting Directions

1. Click the placemark icon to open the address window.

2. Click the "To here" or "From here" link.

3. Enter the desired start or end address.

4. Click the "Go" button.

Additional Options

Refer to the image at the right for more options.

1. Click for reverse directions.

2. Use this link to add an additional destination.

3. Change the method of travel to "public transit" or "walking."

4. View a picture of each step.

5. Click and drag the blue line on the map to change the route. (See images below.)

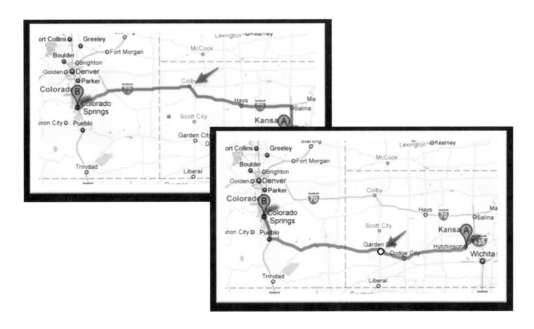

Classroom Activities for Basic Google Maps
Basic Activities – No Google Account required

Find locations on the map and get directions from your school for:

- Cities/states/ countries you encounter during social studies or current events.
- The setting of a book or story.
- The setting of a movie or video.

Practice estimation:

- Students estimate how far it is from _____ to _____ and then use Google Maps to see how close they were.

Students plan an overnight trip to a city within driving distance. They use Google maps to find:

- Driving directions from their home to their destination.
- A hotel for the night.
- One or more places to eat their favorite food.
- Something to do for entertainment. (A movie theater, mall, or amusement park, perhaps.)

Students can find their home or school address on a Google map; switch to the satellite view; and explore their community from a different point of view.

Students can view a map of the U.S.; switch to the terrain view; and explore:

- Name the mountain ranges you see.
- Why is the region in the center of the U.S. called the "plains"?
- Where would be the best places to go snow skiing in the winter?

Advanced Google Maps

My Maps Tools

1. Go to: maps.google.com

2. Sign in using your Google Account.

3. Click the "My Maps" link at the upper left.

4. At the left side of the screen, scroll down to the "Featured Content."

Distance Measurement Tool

1. Zoom in or out, or enter an address to find the desired location on the map.

2. Click the "Distance Measurement" tool in the "Featured content" area.

3. Click the map to establish the starting point for measurement.

4. Click again for each location you want to add to the measurement.

5. When you are finished measuring, make sure you un-check the distance measurement tool at the left side of the screen

   Example: Let's say I want to see how far it would be if I traveled from Kansas, to California, to New York, to Florida, and finally back to Kansas. My map would look like the image at the right.

   At the left side of the screen, you'll see the total distance, and you'll also see buttons that will allow you to delete points and reset the distance measurement tool.

Other Featured Content

You may want to explore some of the other tools in the "Featured Content" area. Google is always adding new features, so check back often!

Custom Google Maps

You can create a custom map with your own place markers, lines, and shapes.

Getting Ready

1. Go to: maps.google.com

2. Sign in using your Google Account.

3. Click the "My Maps" link at the upper-left.

4. Click the "Create New Map" link at the upper-left.

5. Enter a title and description and choose whether you want your map to be public or unlisted.

Adding Markers

1. Zoom in to the desired location.

2. Click to select the placemark icon.

3. Click the desired location on the map to set the marker.

4. Enter a title and description and change the placemark icon, if desired. (Just click the icon and other options will become available.)

5. Click OK.

6. Repeat Steps 1-5 to add additional markers to the map.

7. Use the tools at the top to add lines and shapes if desired.

8. Click "Save" at the left side of the screen.

Note – Switch to the "Rich text" editor to format the text and add images!

Sharing Your Map

1. Click the "Link" button in the upper-right corner.

2. Give the provided link to others to view your map. (See page 139 for tips for sharing a long URL.)

3. Use the provided HTML code to embed your map in a blog, wiki, or website. (See page 48.)

Collaborative Maps

You can allow your students, their parents, or anyone to add placemarks to your map – all at the same time! *Users must have a Google Account to edit a collaborative map.*

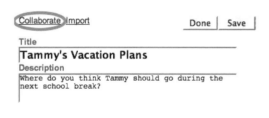

Creating a Collaborative Map

1. Follow the steps on the previous page to create and save a new map.

2. Click the "Collaborate" link at the left side of the screen.

3. In the pop-up window, click to "Allow anyone to edit this map."

4. Follow the "Sharing Your Map" instructions above to share the map with the other map "editors."

Editing a Collaborative Map

Others can edit your map by doing this:

1. Go to the provided URL.

2. Sign in using your Google Account.

3. Click the "Edit" button.

4. Follow the steps on the previous page to add placemarks.

Classroom Activities for Advanced Google Maps

These activities require a Google account.

Use the **distance measurement tool** to:

- Measure the walking route from home to school.

- Plan a 2-mile walking route around your home or the school. (It may help to switch to the satellite view.) (See images at right.)

- Compare: How far is it for a bird to fly from ____ to ____? vs. How far is it to drive from ____ to ____?

- After estimating a distance, use the distance measurement tool to see how close you were.

Distance Measurement Tool

Click on the map to trace a path you want to measure.

Units:
   ○ Metric ⦿ English *I'm feeling geeky*

Total distance:
1.98066 mi

Use the **"My Map"** option, create a new map, and add placemarks to:

- Write a story where you travel to different locations. Put each chapter of your story within a placemark. (See images at the right.)

- Plan a vacation. Create a placemark for each "stop." In the placemark description, tell what you will do at that location. (Could also "map" a vacation you've already taken.)

- Choose a literature book or movie where the characters travel to different locations. Mark the locations on a Google map and add descriptions to the placemarks.

  Book/Movie Ideas:
  "The Grapes of Wrath"
  "So B. It"
  "Around the World in 80 Days"
  "The Adventures of Young Indiana Jones"
  "National Treasure 1 & 2"

Title
The Tornado!
Description

Privacy and sharing settings   *Learn more*

○ **Public** - Shared with everyone. This map will be published in search results and user profiles.

⦿ **Unlisted** - Shared only with selected people who have this map's URL.

Chapter 1
It started as an ordinary day in northwest Kansas. I

Chapter 2
I begrudgingly got in the truck without even looking to

Chapter 3
By the time we got to Hays, the wind was whipping.

Chapter 4
The radio announcer was urging everyone to find

- Create a family tree map. Add placemarks to show the birthplaces of parents, grandparents, great-grandparents, etc.

- Follow and mark the campaign trail of a presidential candidate.

- Track the travels of a friend/relative who is a truck driver, a traveling salesman, or one who is on vacation.

- Zoom in to a map of your community. Students add placemarks for their homes, grocery store, fire station, school, park, swim pool, hospital, etc. (See images at right.)

- Travel wish list – Students add placemarks for all the places they want to visit in their lifetime.

 My Home

 The Swim Pool

 The Elementary School

 The Police Station

 The Hospital

 The Restaurant

 The Grocery Store

- Track a favorite musician or band on tour. Mark each of their concert stops and share a couple of interesting facts about that city.

- Follow the television show "The Amazing Race" and mark the location of each challenge.

Use a **collaborative map** for these activities:

- Birthplaces – Each student adds a placemark to show where they were born.

- 50 States Research
  Each student is assigned 2 or 3 states. On a collaborative map, he/she adds a placemark on the state that includes the state name, the capital, 3 additional facts, and maybe even a picture of the state flag!

- Create a tourism map for your state or community. Add placemarks and descriptions for must-see attractions for visitors.

- Choose a State
Prompt "If you could live in any
state/country, which would you choose?"
Each student adds a placemark in his or her
chosen state or country. (Students will enter
their name in the title field and enter their
justification in the description area.) (See
images at the right.)

- What State Am I?
Each student adds a placemark to the map.
The teacher gives a clue, and the students
move their placemark to show their guess.
The teacher continues to give clues until all
students' markers are in the right state.

Example clues for Colorado:
- I'm in the United States.
- I have mountains.
- My capital is called the mile high city.
- One of my bordering states is Wyoming.
- The Broncos play football here.
- I start with the letter "C."

What state would you choose?
Table 6
Privacy and sharing settings Learn more

- **Public** - Shared with everyone. This map will be published in search results and user profiles.
- **Unlisted** - Shared only with selected people who have this map's URL.

 Todd
I'd live in Hawaii where the weather is warm year

 Lacey
I want to lay on the beach and soak up the sun ar

 John
I'd live in North Dakota because I love the cold an

 TJ
I'd choose Floria, so I could go to Disney World

Blogger
Google's Blog Tool

Want to create a blog to share your teaching experiences.? How about a weekly newsletter for parents? A daily journal for students? Well – Blogger is the tool for you!

The word "blog" sounds scary, but it's not. It is actually the mashup of two words: web + log = blog. Google's Blogger tool is so easy to use that you can create a new blog and publish your first post within 5 minutes. No kidding! Try it yourself and see…

Blogger
Google's Blog Tool

Creating a Sandbox Blog

For your first attempt, let's create a "sandbox" blog – one that you can practice and experiment with…

Getting Started

1. Go to: www.blogger.com

2. Sign in using your Google account. (If you need help setting up and account, see page 133.)

3. Click the "Create Your Blog Now" arrow or the "Create a Blog" link at the top-right corner of the page.

4. Enter a blog title. The title will appear at the top of your blog. Enter a title like "Tammy's Sandbox Blog."

5. Choose and enter a blog address. This is the address that visitors will use to get to your blog. Do not include odd symbols or spaces.

    Enter something like "twsandbox" to create a blog address (URL) of: http://twsandbox.blogger.com.

6. Complete the word verification and then click the Continue arrow.

7. Choose a template that you like and then click the Continue arrow. (Don't worry – you can always change it later.)

8. Click the "Start Blogging" arrow.

Create a **blog** in **3** easy steps:

1. Create an account
2. Name your blog
3. Choose a template

CREATE YOUR BLOG NOW

Name your blog

Blog title	Tammy's Sandbox Blog
	Your blog's title will appear on you
Blog address (URL)	http://twsandbox
	Check Availability

2. Choose a **template**

Posting to Your Blog

After you click the "Start Blogging" arrow, you'll be ready to enter your first post.

1. In the title field, enter "Welcome."

2. In the body (message) area, enter a welcome message.

3. Click the "Publish Post" button at the bottom of the screen.

4. Click the "View Blog" link to see your creation!

Blogger Views/Modes

There are three main areas for viewing/editing your blogs: The Published Blog, The Edit Mode, and the Dashboard.

1. **The Published Blog**

   To get to the published blog, do one of the following:
   - Enter the URL. (http://twsandbox.blogspot.com)

   - While in the Edit Mode, click the "View Blog" link at the top of the page.

   - From the Dashboard, click the "View Blog" link under your blog title.

2. **The Edit Mode**
   This is where you will change the settings and layout options for your blog.

To get to the edit mode, do one of the following:
- From the Published Blog view, click the "Customize" link at the top-right corner, or click the pencil icon beside a blog post.

- From the Dashboard view, click the "Settings" link below your blog title.

3. **The Dashboard**
   This is where you can see and access all of the blogs you have created using Blogger.

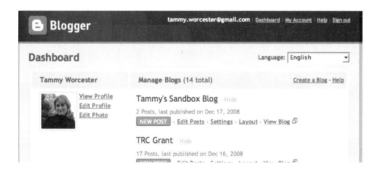

To get to the Dashboard, do one of the following:
- Enter the URL: www.blogger.com

- From the Edit view, click the "Dashboard" link in the upper-right corner.

Exploring the Blog Screen (Published Blog Mode)

1. Click the "New Post" link to create additional posts.

2. Click the "Customize" link to switch to the edit mode for your blog.

3. Viewers will click the "Comments" button to view and/or add comments.

4. Click the pencil icon to edit the post. This also switches you to the edit mode for your blog.

5. Click the tool icon to edit or remove the information at the side of your blog.

Exploring the "Customize" Screen (Edit Mode)

1. The three tabs at the upper-left allow you to edit posts, change settings, and customize the layout of your blog. (We'll learn more about that later.)

2. Click the "View Blog" link to switch to the Published Blog view.

3. Click the "Dashboard" link to switch to the Dashboard view.

Exploring the Dashboard Screen

1. Click one of the links at the left to view or edit your profile or to edit your photo.

   This profile will be associated with all blogs you create and with any comments you make on blogs created by others.

2. Click the "Create a Blog" link at the upper-right corner of the screen to create a new blog.

3. Click the links under any blog title to:
   • Create a new post
   • Edit posts
   • Go to the Settings area
   • Go to the Layout area
   • View the blog

Customizing/Editing Your Blog

There are hundreds of options for customizing your blog. Just click through the tabs and links in the Edit mode and you'll see. We're going to explore a few of the custom options you might want to try. *Make sure you are in the Edit Mode.*

Editing Posts

To delete a post

1. Click the "Posting" tab, then the "Edit Posts" link.

2. Find the post you want to delete.

3. Click the "Delete" button at the right of your post title.

To change the date/time of a post
(This might also change the order of your published posts, as the most recent posts are published at the top of the blog.)

1. Click the "Posting" tab, then the "Edit Posts" link.

2. Find the desired post and click the "Edit" button.

3. Click the "Post Options" link at the bottom of the screen.

4. Enter the desired date and time.

To publish or save as draft

1. Click the "Publish Post" button to publish a post.

2. Click the "Save as Draft" button if you want to publish it later.

   Note – If your post is already published, the "Save as Draft" button will un-publish it and turn it into a draft.

Custom Settings

Make sure you are in the Edit mode, and then click the Settings Tab.

To change the number of posts that will show on your main blog page:

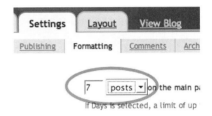

1. Click the "Formatting" link at the top of the page.

2. In the "Show" field, enter the desired number of posts.

To customize comments:

If allowed, viewers can add comments to each blog post.

1. Click the "Comments" link at the top of the page.

2. In the "Who Can Comment?" area, click to determine who can comment to posts on your blog.

3. In the "Comment Form Placement" area, click to determine where you want the comment window to appear.

Who Can Comment?

- Anyone - *Includes Anonymous Users*
- Registered Users - *Includes OpenID*
- Users with Google Accounts
- Only members of this blog

Comment Form Placement

- Full page
- Pop-up window
- Embedded below post

To moderate comments:

The "Moderate Comments" option gives you the opportunity to view and approve viewer's comments before they are published to your blog.

1. Click the "Comments" link at the top of the page.

2. In the "Comment Moderation" area, click to choose "Always" if you want to moderate comments, or click "Never" if you don't want to moderate comments.

If you choose "Always", enter your email address. Now when a viewer adds a comment, you will receive an email. Within the email message, you can read the comment and then choose whether to publish or reject it.

Comment Moderation

- Always
- Only on posts older than [14] days
- Never

Review comments before they are published. dashboard when there are comments to revie

Email address

_____

We will email you at this address when a non your blog. Leave blank if you don't want to re

Anonymous has left a new commer

I love your blog!

Publish this comment.

Reject this comment.

Moderate comments for this blog.

Custom Layout

Make sure you are in the Edit mode, and then click the Layout Tab.

To add and/or arrange page elements:

1. Click the "Page Elements" link at the top of the page.

2. Click and drag elements to rearrange them.

3. Click the "Edit" link on any page element to change or remove it.

4. Click the "Preview" button at the top right to view your changes. Click the "Save" button when finished.

To add gadgets:

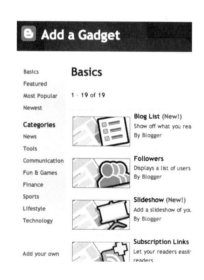

1. Click the "Page Elements" link at the top of the page.

2. Click one of the "Add a Gadget" links.

3. In the "Add a Gadget" window, click the categories at the left and browse the gadgets at the right.

4. Click the blue "plus sign" button to add the desired gadget.

   Here are some gadgets you might want to include at the side of your blog:

Picture
Use the "Picture" gadget to add a photo or a clip art.

Text
Add a "Text" gadget if you want to add a blog description, a welcome message, or instructions for reading the blog.

Subscription Links
If you want to give others the opportunity to subscribe to your blog with Google Reader (see page 61) or another RSS feed reader, add the "Subscription Links" gadget.

To edit blog post options:

1. Click the "Page Elements" link at the top of the page.

2. Click the "Edit" link in the "Blog Posts" area.

3. Click the check boxes to select the items you want to be displayed on each blog post.

4. At the bottom of the window, click and drag the items to arrange them in the desired positions.

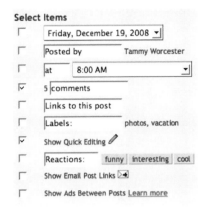

To change to a different template:

1. Click the "Pick New Template" link.
   Note – There are multiple options within some of the templates. In the image at the right, for example, you can see that there are four different "denim" choices.

2. Click to choose the template style you want, then click the "Save" button.

To change fonts and colors:

1. Click the "Fonts and Colors" link at the top of the page.

2. In the window at the left, scroll to see the color for each element in your blog. Click to choose the element you want to change.

3. Use the color palette or font palette at the right to select a new color or font.

4. Repeat for each element you want to customize.

5. View the changes using the preview screen at the bottom of the page.

6. Click the "Save" button when finished.

Four Ways to Post to your Blog

Once you've set up your blog using Google's Blogger tool, you can add posts in a variety of ways.

Option 1 – Posting Via Blogger

1. Go to www.blogger.com and click the "New Post" button under your blog title.

   or

Tammy's Sandbox Blog

1 Post, last published on Dec 1

[NEW POST] - Edit Posts - Set

2. Go to your blog's address (http://twsandbox.blogspot.com) and click the "New Post" link in the top-right corner of the screen.

To fancy-up your post:
(See image below)

1. Use the provided tools to change the fonts, styles, sizes, and alignment and to add hyperlinks.

2. Click the picture icon and follow the on-screen prompts to add an image.

3. Click the video icon and follow the on-screen prompts to add a video.

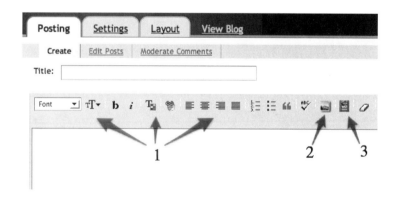

Option 2 – Posting from Google Docs

(See pages 109–112 to see how to use Google Documents.)

1. Open a Google Document and enter the desired message.

2. Pull down the "Share" menu to "Publish as web page."

3. Click the "Publish to blog" button.

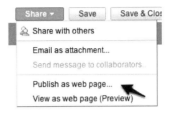

Option 3 – Posting Via iGoogle

(See page 19 for iGoogle instructions.)

1. Find the Blogger gadget and add it to your iGoogle page.

2. If you have more than one blog, choose the one you want from the pull-down menu.

3. Enter the title and body for your post.

4. Click the "Publish" button.

5. Once the publishing process is finished, click the "View Blog" link to see your published post!

45

Option 4 – Email from Computer

1. Go to the Edit mode of your blog to set up the email option:

2. Click the "Settings" tab and then the "Email" link:

3. Enter the desired mail-to address; click the "Save Settings" button. *Be sure to enter something that will identify this particular blog. No spaces or symbols!*

4. Go to your email client and compose your email.
   Note - The email subject will become the title of the post, and the email message will become the body of the post.

5. Send the message and then check your blog to see if the post is there!

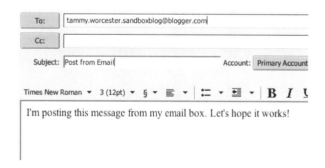

Bonus! Attach a photo to your email and it will be posted in your blog message!

Option 5 – Email from Cell Phone/Mobile Device

If your cell phone (or any other mobile device) has email capabilities, you can easily add posts to your blog! (See the previous post "Email from Computer" to learn the basic steps.)

You'll need to consult a user's manual (or ask a teenager) if you don't know how to send an email from your phone. Here's how it works on an iPhone:

1. Take a picture using the iPhone Camera.

2. Click the "share" link; choose the "Email Photo" option.

3. Address the message to the "mail to" address you created on the previous page.

4. Enter a subject and a message.

5. Click the "Send" button.

Wait a couple of minutes (maybe even seconds) and check your blog to see your new post!

Using Embed Code in Your Blog Posts

Many web tools are available that will allow you to create a "widget" and then embed it into your blog. First we'll go through the basic steps. Then we'll look at individual web tools in more detail.

Basic Steps

1. Use a web tool (see the options below and on the following pages) to generate embed code.

2. Copy the provided embed code.

3. Go to the "Post Message" area for your blog or go to your iGoogle page and use your Blogger widget.

4. Paste the embed code in the message area of the blog post.

5. Publish your blog post.

Google Widgets For Your Blog

Google Maps

1. Go to: www.maps.google.com

2. Create a map. (This can be a basic map, a custom map, or a collaborative map.) See pages 23-32 for instructions.

3. Click the "Link" button in the upper-right corner.

4. Copy the provided HTML embed code.

5. Paste the code into a new blog post; publish the post!

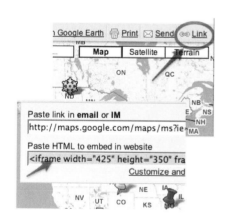

Google Forms

1. Go to: docs.google.com

2. Create a form. (See page 125 for instructions.)

3. In the upper-right corner, click the "More actions" link and choose "Embed."

4. Copy the provided HTML embed code.

5. Paste the code into a new blog post; publish the post!

   Now viewers can complete and submit the form right in your blog! The results will show in your spreadsheet at docs.google.com.

Google Calendar

1.   Go to: www.google.com/calendar

2.   Create a calendar. (See pages 79- 85 for instructions.)

3.   At the left side of the calendar, in the "My calendars" area, click the pull-down arrow beside the calendar name.

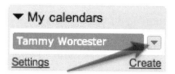

4.   From the pull-down menu, choose "Calendar Settings."

5.   Locate the "Embed This Calendar" options.

6.   Click the "Customize…" link to change the color, size, and other options.

7.   Copy the provided HTML embed code.

8.   Paste the code into a new blog post; publish the post!

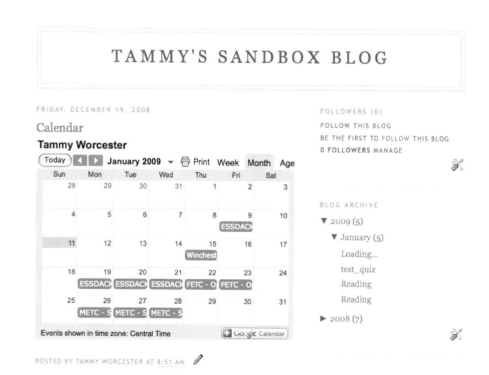

Other Widgets For Your Blog

Listed below are some non-Google widgets you can embed into your blog. Basic instructions are included. For more specific directions, see the help or FAQ area for each tool.

Video from TeacherTube or YouTube

You can easily embed a video into your blog. Maybe it is a video created by your students. Or maybe you want your students to watch someone else's video and then post comments...

1. Go to: www.teachertube.com or www.youtube.com

2. Find the desired video.

3. Copy the provided embed code and paste it into your blog post.

▼ Embed Video | ▶ Related Videos & Tags

URL: http://www.teachertube.com/view_video.
(E-mail or link it.)

Large Screen URL: http://www.teachertube.com/v.php?viewk
(E-mail or link it.)

Embeddable w/ Video Search: <embed src="http://www.teachertube.co
NEW (SEE EXAMPLE HERE.This embeddable player has a built-in TeacherTube Video Search Bar! Put this video on your website. Works on PBwiki, PMwiki, Wikispaces, Friendster, Blogger, MySpace!)

Embeddable w/out Video Search: <embed src="http://www.teachertube.co
(This is the original embeddable player. Put this video on your website. Works on PBwiki, PMwiki, Wikispaces, Friendster, Blogger, MySpace!)

Delicious Links

Bookmark a website with delicious, and the link will automatically be added to your blog!

1. Go to: www.delicious.com

2. Log on to your Delicious account.

3. Click the "Settings" link.

4. Click the "Link Rolls" link.

5. Follow the on-screen prompts to set up your link roll.

6. Copy the provided code and paste it into your blog post.

Links for Art Teachers & Students:
- Sumopaint.com beta - Image Editing in
- Interactive and Instructional Sites for I
- Dabbleboard - A powerful and easy-to-
- art.com artPad
- string spin toy - zefrank.com
- 2D Animation | Computer Animation So
- Imagination Cubed
- Right Brain vs Left Brain Creativity Tes
- Make-a-Flake - A snowflake maker by B
- Picnik - edit photos the easy way, onlir
- National Gallery of Art NGA Kids Art Zo
- DrawerGeeks!
- National Gallery of Art | NGAkids home

Voki

Create a talking avatar and add it to your blog!

1. Go to: http://www.voki.com/

2. No login is necessary, but if you want to edit an avatar later, you'll need to create an account.

3. Follow the on-screen prompts to create an avatar and add a "voice."

4. Copy the provided embed code and paste it into your blog post.

Flickr

Display a slide show of Flickr photos right in your blog!

1. Go to: www.flickr.com

2. Create a Flickr (Yahoo) account/log in.

3. Upload the desired photos to Flickr.

4. Create a set.

5. Open the set as a slide show.

6. Within the slide show area, click the "Share" button.

7. Copy the provided code and paste it into your blog post.

SlideShare

Share a PowerPoint presentation right in your blog!

1. Go to: www.slideshare.net

2. Create a PowerPoint presentation and upload it to SlideShare, or choose a presentation that has already been uploaded to SlideShare.

3. Copy the provided embed code from SlideShare and paste it into your blog post.

ISSUU

Create your own eBook (from any pdf file) that can be easily accessed from your blog. Could be used for teacher handouts or for the e-publishing of student work.

1. Go to: www.issuu.com

2. Create an account/log in.

3. Upload a pdf.

4. Check your email. A message will be sent when your ebook is ready. Click the link in your email to see the ebook.

5. Make any desired changes.

6. Copy the provided code and paste it into your blog post.

7. In the blog, viewers can click to turn the pages of the ebook.

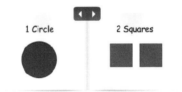

Poll Daddy

Create a poll to gather responses from students, parents, or other viewers and immediately see the results!

1. Go to: http://www.polldaddy.com

2. Create an account/log in.

3. Follow the on-screen prompts to create a new poll.

4. Copy the provided code and paste it into your Blogger post.

5. In the blog, viewers vote on their choice and they will immediately see the results of the voting!

USTREAM

Embed live video from your computer's camera or a web camera. Stream a teacher lesson or student presentations for the whole world to view!

1. Go to: http://www.ustream.tv/

2. Create an account/log in.

3. Create a new show.

4. Copy the provided embed code for the video and/or the chat.

5. Paste the code in your Blogger post.

    Note – You can use the same ustream "show" each time you want to stream video into your blog. Whenever you are broadcasting, viewers can watch right on your blog!

Image from www.kevinhoneycutt.com

Cover It Live

Cover It Live lets you and/or students live-blog a class or event.

1. Go to: www.coveritlive.com

2. Create an account/log in.

3. Follow the on-screen prompts to create a new live blog.

4. Copy the provided embed code.

5. Paste the code into your blog post.

    Now when you "cover" a class or event, viewers can read the notes in your blog!

Random Name Picker

Let the computer randomly choose a student's from a list!

1. Go to:
   http://www.classtools.net/main_area/fruit_machine.htm

2. Enter your students' names.

3. Click the embed button in the bottom right corner.
   (Looks like a wheel.)

4. Copy the provided code and paste it into your blog
   post.

5. Within the blog, click the "Fruit Machine" or the
   "Typewriter" button to pick a student's name.

   Note – Don't give up if the embed code doesn't work
   on the first try. Just repeat the steps and try again!

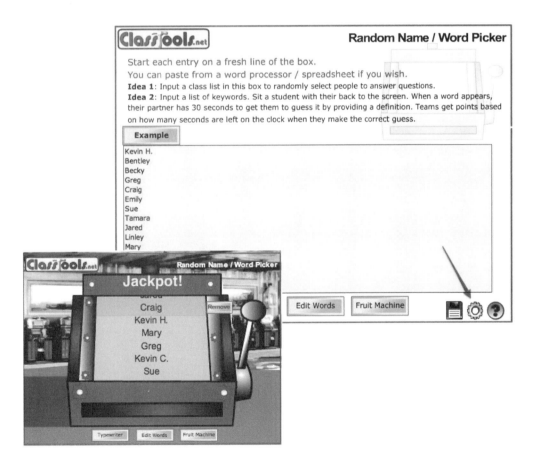

A Blog Within a Blog (A Blidget)

Want a nice way to organize multiple sets of information in a blog post? How about creating a blog within a blog?

Let's say you have a class newsletter blog (Blog A) where you post news and pictures from your classroom. Your students write some amazing holiday stories and you want to publish those to your newsletter blog. You could put all of the student stories together into **one** blog post, but that would be difficult to navigate. Or you could create a **different** blog post for each story – but that would take a LOT of screen space.

The blog within a blog solution provides an easier method – and it allows the teacher, parents, and others to add comments to individual student stories.

1. Create a second blog (Blog B) and add a new post for each student's story. (If you have 20 students, Blog B will have 20 posts.)

2. Go to:
   http://www.widgetbox.com/make_blidget.jsp

3. Follow the online prompts to turn Blog B into a widget (actually called a "blidget.") You will need a widgetbox account/login for this step. (It is free!)

4. Click the "Get Widget" button; copy the provided embed code.

5. Paste the embed code into a post in your classroom blog (Blog A).

6. In Blog A, viewers can click the "Holiday Stories" title to see all student stories, or they can click the student's name to see an individual story.

One more cool thing – when new posts are added to the "Holiday Stories" blog, they are automatically added to the blidget!

Make a Blidget

Take your blog or feed.   Make it into a widget.

4th Grade Nothings!

Sunday, December 14, 2008
4th Grade Holiday Stories
Click a student's name below to view his / her story:

Holiday Stories

Recent Posts
TJ
Jordan
Todd
John
Mary

Classroom Blog Ideas

You can combine some of these ideas into a single blog, or you can create a number of different blogs for different purposes. Note – make sure you get permission from parents before sharing student work or photos online.

Teacher Blogs

- **Weekly Newsletter**
  Instead of (or in addition to) sending home a paper newsletter, do it as a blog. Just let the parents know the URL and they can check it regularly.

- **Sharing Student Work**
  Share student drawings, writing, voice recordings, and pictures of students in the classroom through a blog.

- **Spelling Lists**
  Use a blog to post your spelling lists or vocabulary lists for the week.

- **Teaching Tips**
  Create a blog to share teaching tips and ideas with other teachers.

- **A Blog of Widgets**
  Create a blog to "house" a random name picker widget for each of your classes. (See page 56 for instructions.)

- **Resources for Parents**
  Post lists of websites, books, TV shows, movies, hands-on manipulatives and other resources that would help to expand the learning beyond the classroom.

- **Feedback from Parents**
  Post a question or prompt, and let parents add comments to your blog post. Or – embed a Google Form into your blog to gather information from parents. (See page 125 for instructions.)

- **Lesson Plans**
  Post your lesson plans for the week in a blog for administrators and/or parents to view.

- **Absent Student Info**
  Have a student who is absent? Post the assignments for the day, post a PowerPoint presentation or two, or even USTREAM a lesson.

Teacher/Student Blogs

These blogs are set up by the teacher, so they do not require student Google accounts.

- **Daily Journal**
  Post a prompt or question each day to your blog. Students can add a comment to answer the question or to respond to the prompt.

- **Reading Response Journal**
  Post questions for a book or story you are reading as a class and let students add comments to respond.

- **Online Debate**
  Ask a challenging question or post a provocative prompt and then let students add comments with their arguments or justifications.

- **Gathering Data**
  Use a Google Form within your blog to gather data from students during or after a science experiment. Then go to the spreadsheet to analyze the data.

- **Online Voting**
  Embed a Google Form or a Poll Daddy questionnaire into your blog to vote for class president, to decide where to go on a field trip, or to choose the next book to read as a class.

- **Photo Essays**
  Create a "happiness" blog. Provide the "mail-to" email address to post to the blog. (See page 44 for instructions.)

  Students can use their cell phone or a digital camera to take a photo of something that represents happiness to them. They will email their photo (along with a description) to the blog.

  This idea can be used with a variety of different concepts: hope, prejudice, generosity, selfishness, selflessness, freedom, etc.

  Younger students could post pictures of: something green; something that contains a circle or triangle; something healthy to eat; something with four legs; etc.

Google Reader

You've probably discovered some interesting blogs about teaching and learning, and maybe some websites that provide the latest educational news, or even recipes or home decorating tips. But – do you have time to check them every day to see if there's something new? Do you remember to check them?

If the answer is no to either of the questions above, Google Reader may be just what you need!

Google Reader allows you to "subscribe" to blogs or websites that are frequently updated and then it lets you know when something new has been added!

Common Craft has produced a great video that explains how Google Reader works. You can view it at: www.commoncraft.com/rss_plain_english

Google Reader

Getting Started

1. Go to: www.google.com/reader

2. Sign in using your Google Account information.

   That's really all you need to do in the Google Reader area. Now you're ready to add some subscriptions.

Adding Subscriptions

1. Go to one of your favorite blogs.
   If you can't think of one, you can go to:
   tipofweek.tammyworcester.com

2. Locate and click the "RSS" or "Subscribe" button. Depending on what browser you are using, use one of the following options:

   a. If you see a page that looks like Image A at the right, click the "Add to Google Reader" button.

   b. If you see a page that looks like Image B, click the "Add to Google" button.

   c. If you see a page of text or code, do the following:

      i. Copy the URL in the address window.

      ii. Go to: www.google.com/reader

      iii. In Google Reader, click the "Add Subscription" button in the upper-left corner.

      iv. Paste the URL into the provided window.

3. Repeat steps 1 and 2 for each subscription you want to add.

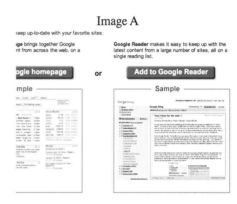

Image A

Image B

Finding Blogs

You might want to ask your colleagues for recommendations of blogs to follow, or you can use these resources to discover some great blogs on your own:

- **Google Blog Search**
  http://blogsearch.google.com/
  Browse blogs by category, or search for blogs of interest.

- **Technorati**
  http://technorati.com
  Search for blogs by keyword, or browse the lists of new, popular, and favorite blogs.

- **The Edublog Awards**
  http://edublogawards.com/
  Browse lists of the best educational blogs.

When you find a blog you like, be sure to subscribe to it, so it will appear in your Google Reader.

Reading New Posts

1. Go to: www.google.com/reader

2. A quick look at the left side of the screen will show you if new information has been added to any of your subscriptions. (The number in parenthesis shows how many new posts there are.)

3. Click the title of one of your subscriptions to view the new information.

4. Scroll through the items and read them inside Google Reader, or click the double arrow to open the original website.

5. As you scroll through the items, they will be marked as read. You can also click the "Mark all as read" button if you want.

Organizing Subscriptions with Folders

When you get some subscriptions in your reader, you may want to organize them into folders:

1. Go to: www.google.com/reader

2. Click the "Manage subscriptions" link in the bottom-left corner of the screen.

3. Here you will see a list of all of your subscriptions. Click the "Add to a folder" button and pull down to "New folder."

4. Enter a name for your new folder.

5. To add other subscriptions to that folder, click the "Add to a folder" button and pull down to the name of the folder you just created.

6. Repeat these steps to create additional folders and file your subscriptions.

Organizing Subscriptions with Tags

Another way to organize your subscriptions is to add tags. Tags are key words or labels you attach to an item. Later, you can easily find all items with the same tag.

1. Go to: www.google.com/reader

2. Find an item in your reader that you would like to tag.

3. At the bottom of the item, click the "Add tags" button.

4. Enter the tag(s) you want. If you enter more than one, separate the tags with a comma.

5. To find your tagged items:

   a. Locate the "Subscriptions" window at the left side of the screen and scroll to the bottom.

   b. Click to select the desired tag.

   c. All items with the selected tag will show in the main window.

Starred Items

When you find a blog post that you particularly like, or one that you want to return to again, you can "star" it so that you can find it again easily.

1. Go to: www.google.com/reader

2. Click a subscription title and find an entry that you really like.

3. Click the star at the left of the title.

4. To view your "favorite" items, click the "Starred items" link at the left side of the screen.

Removing Subscriptions

1. Go to: www.google.com/reader

2. Click the "Manage subscriptions" link in the bottom-left corner of the screen.

3. Click to put a check box in front of the title(s) you want to remove.

4. Click the "Unsubscribe" button.

Marking Items to Share

1. Go to: www.google.com/reader

2. Find an item that you would like to share.

3. At the bottom of the item, click the "Share" or "Share with note" button.

Sharing Items from Google Reader

After marking some items to share (see instructions above), you can easily share them with others.

1. Click the "Shared items" button at the left side of the screen.

2. To share as a web page:

    a. In the main window, choose a style for your shared items page.

    b. Click the provided link to get the URL for your shared items page.

    c. Share the URL with your friends, colleagues, students, parents, etc.
        (See page 139 for tips for sharing a long URL.)

3. To share via email:

    a. Click the "Email" link.

    b. Enter the email address or addresses of your friends, colleagues, students, parents, etc.

    c. Click OK.

        The recipients will receive an email with a link to your shared items page.

4. To embed your shared items in your blog:

    a. Click the "Add a clip" link.

    b. Click the "Add to Blogger" button to add your shared items to the side of your blog.

        or

        Copy and paste the provided code to add your shared items to a blog post. (See page 48 for instructions.)

Google Reader in iGoogle

You can view your Google Reader subscriptions on your iGoogle page!

1. Go to: www.google.com; Click the "iGoogle" link at the upper-right.

2. Add the "Google Reader" gadget. (See page 19 for instructions.)

3. In the Google Reader gadget:

   a. Choose the desired folder from the pull-down menu at the top.

   b. Click a title to read the new post in a pop-up window.

   c. Click the "mark all is read" link to "clean up" your reader.

   d. Click the "Google Reader" title at the top of the gadget to go to your Google Reader page.

Search results for "google reader"

Google Reader
View your Google Reader any RSS or Atom feed.
http://www.google.com/

Add it now

Google Reader: Ed Tech (11)

Ed Tech (11) ▾   refresh   mark all as read

Games Sell
from 2¢ Worth
This is Why I Built Class Blogmeister
from 2¢ Worth
Just Numbers
from 2¢ Worth
Come Along Inside…
from 2¢ Worth
They're Telling the Wrong Story Again…
from 2¢ Worth

Google Notebook

Remember the stack of 3 x 5 cards we used for keeping track of our resources for a research paper? Well, now that can all be done electronically – using a tool like Google Notebook.

With Google Notebook, you can "clip" text, images and links as you browse the Internet, and then and easily organize your "clippings."

Google Notebook

Getting Started

1. Go to: www.google.com/notebook

2. Sign in using your Google Account.

Installing the Browser Buttons
To use Google Notebook efficiently, you'll need to install a browser extension:

If you are using Firefox or Internet Explorer,

1. Go to: www.google.com/notebook/download

2. Follow the on-screen prompts to download and install the extension.

3. Locate the "Open Notebook" button in the very bottom-right corner of your browser window

   or

   Locate the "Notebook" button in the Google Toolbar at the top of your browser window.

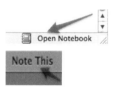

If you are using Safari or any other browser (or if you can't get the above method to work with Firefox or Internet Explorer):

1. Go to: http://www.google.com/googlenotebook/ bookmarklet.html

2. Follow the on-screen prompts to move the "Note This" bookmarklet into your bookmarks bar.

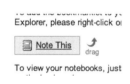

3. Locate the "Note This" button in your bookmarks bar at the top of the screen.

Setting Up Notebooks

Let's say you want to do some research and find some
current information for some units you're getting ready
to teach. One of the units covers nutrition, and the other
will be about zoo animals. Let's set up a notebook for
each. (Of course, you can substitute any topics you
want for "nutrition" and "zoo animals.")

1. Go to: www.google.com/notebook

2. Click the "Create a new notebook" link.

3. Name the notebook, "Nutrition."

4. Click OK.

5. Repeat to create a notebook named "Zoo Animals."

6. Now you're ready to start adding information to
    your notebooks.

Clipping Information

Do a Google Search to find information about nutrition.
When you find information you want to save, use one
of the following methods to "clip" it.

In Firefox or Internet Explorer

1. Select the text and/or image you want to clip.

2. Open the mini-notebook using one of these options:

    •   Click the "Open Notebook" button in the
        bottom-right corner of your Firefox browser.

    •   Click the "Notebook" icon in your Google
        Toolbar in Internet Explorer.

    •   Click the right mouse button and choose, "Note
        This (Google Notebook)."

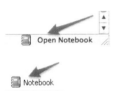

3. In the mini-notebook window, choose the Nutrition
    notebook at the left side.

4. Click the "Clip" icon.

    This will add the selection to your Google
    notebook!

In Safari or Other Browsers:

1. Select the text and/or image you want to "clip."

2. Click the "Note This" button in the bookmarks toolbar at the top of the browser window. This will open a mini-notebook window.

3. In the mini notebook window, click the "Yes, add note" button to confirm that you want to add it.

    This will add the selection to your Google notebook!

Organizing/Editing Clippings (Notes)

*   Click and drag the left edge of a clipping to move it up or down in the list.

*   If a clipping is in the wrong notebook, click the left edge and drag it onto the correct notebook title at the left side of the screen.

*   To delete a clipping, click the triangle in the upper-right corner and pull down to "Delete."
    or
    Click the left edge of a clipping and drag it to the trash can at the left side of the screen.

*   Collapse/Expand individual notes by clicking the +/- button at the left edge.

*   To collapse/expand all notes, click the "Tool" menu in the upper-right corner of the screen and pull down to "Collapse all notes" or "Expand all notes."

*   Add comments or labels by clicking the appropriate icon at the bottom of each clipping.

*   Click between two clippings to add your own notes, or click the "New Note" button at the top of the window.

*   Click and drag to select a portion of text and then use the editing tools at the top of the window to add highlighting, change fonts, sizes and styles, change alignment, etc.

Organizing with Labels

Another way to organize your notes is to add labels.
Later, you can easily find all notes with the same
label.

1. Find an item in your notebook to which you
   want to add a label.

2. At the bottom of the item, click the "Add labels"
   button.

   Email   Keep unread   Add tags

3. Enter the label(s) you want. If you enter more
   than one, separate the labels with a comma.

4. To find your labeled items, locate the "Labels"
   window at the left side of the screen; click to
   select the desired label.

   Labels
   fun (1)
   game (2)
   health (2)
   nutrition (3)

5. All items with the selected label will show in the
   main window.

Collaborating with Others

You can invite other collaborators who will be able
to view, add to, and edit the notebook.

1. Click to choose the desired notebook.

2. Click the "Sharing Options" link at the upper-
   right corner of the main window.

   Invite Collaborators:
   Collaborators may view and edit this notebook. If you ad
   does not have a Google account, we'll help them set one

   Separate email addresses with commas.

3. Enter the email address or addresses for your
   friends, colleagues, or students that you want to
   be collaborators.

4. Click the "Save Settings" button.

   Recipients will receive an email with
   instructions for accessing and collaborating on
   your notebook.

5. You can easily tell which of your notebooks
   have additional collaborators. Just look for the
   "people" icon to the left of the notebook title.

Nutrition
Zoo Animals

Exporting Your Notebook to Google Docs

1. Click to choose the desired notebook.

2. From the "Tools" menu in the upper-right corner, pull down to "Export to Google Docs."

3. Your notebook items will now open in a Google document where you can edit them further. (See pages 109-112 for instructions.)

Publishing Your Notebook as a Web Page

1. Click to choose the desired notebook.

2. From the "Tools" menu in the upper-right corner, pull down to "Export as HTML."

3. A new window or tab will open with your published notebook. The URL at the top will be the address for your notebook.

4. Share the URL with your friends, colleagues, students, parents, etc. (See page 139 for tips for sharing a long URL.)

Google Notebook in iGoogle

You can view your Google Notebook items in your iGoogle page!

1. Go to www.google.com and then click the "iGoogle" link at the upper-right.

2. Add the "Google Notebook" gadget. (See page 19 for instructions.)

3. In the Google Notebook gadget:

   a. Click the left edge of the gadget to switch to a different notebook or to create a new notebook.

   b. Pull down the "Tools" menu to expand or collapse notes or to delete a selected note.

Google Notebook Ideas for Teachers

- **Student Resources**

  Google Notebook provides an easy way to create list of links for students. Just create a new notebook for each content area and then "clip" appropriate websites. Add notes (optional), publish each notebok as a web page, and then share the URLs with your students. (For tips for sharing a long URL, see page 139.)

  Bonus – as you clip additional resources, they will be automatically added to the published page.

Making a Table of Contents Page

After you have generated a web page for each content area (see instructions above), you can create a table of contents page with links to each of them.

1. Create a new notebook named "Student Resources."

2. Open the math resources web page that you published earlier.

3. Clip it to your "Student Resources" notebook.

4. Repeat steps 2 and 3 for all of your content pages.

5. Publish the "Student Resources" notebook as a web page. Share the URL with your students. (See pages 139 for tips for sharing a long URL.)

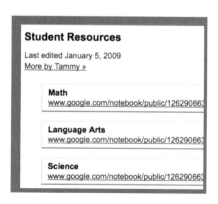

- **Sharing Resources with Other Teachers (or Parents)**

  Maybe you meet with an after-school study group. Or perhaps you team-teach with others. Google Notebook is an easy way to share resources with other teachers. You can even add notes so they will know how to use each resource.

  1. Clip the resources you want to share.

  2. Add notes. (optional)

  3. Publish the notebook as a website. (See previous pages for directions.)

  4. Share the URL with other teachers. (For tips for sharing a long URL, see page 139.)

- **Scavenger Hunts**

  Use Google Notebook to create scavenger hunts for your students.

  1. Create a new notebook with your scavenger hunt title.

  2. Clip the desired resources.

  3. Use the notes area to add instructions or a prompt for each resource.

  4. Publish the notebook as a web page.

  5. Provide the URL to your students. (See page 139 for tips for sharing a long URL.)

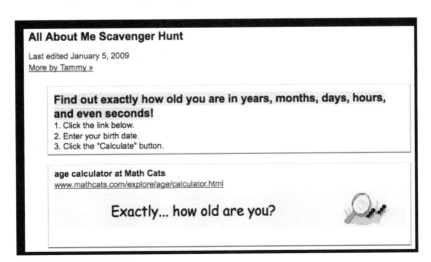

Google Notebook Ideas for Students

Note – Students will need to have a Google Account to set up and maintain Google notebooks.

- **Research**

  Students can gather, store, and organize their online resources for a term paper or project. They can even add notes from offline resources.

- **Collaborative Research**

  Students working together on projects can share in the gathering of information.

- **Student-Created Hotlists**

  Let older students create "hotlists" of resources for younger students. It is a great content review for your students and can save the other teachers tons of time.

  1. Contact the teachers of lower grades in your school or district and compile a list of topics they will be teaching in the near future.

  2. Let your students choose a topic (or two) from the list.

  3. Students create and publish a Google Notebook with resources for each topic.

  4. Provide the published notebook URLs to the lower-grade teachers.

Google Calendar

Use Google Calendar to organize your busy schedule and keep track of events.

Afraid you'll forget something? Google Calendar will send you an email reminder.

You can easily share your calendar with others and you can post it to your blog or web page!

Google Calendar

Getting Started

1. Go to: www.google.com/calendar

2. Sign in using your Google Account.

3. Follow the onscreen prompts to set up a calendar.

Exploring the Screen

1. Click the left/right facing triangles to move forward or backward through the calendar. Click the "Today" button to select the current date on the calendar.

2. Click the "Print" button to print the current view of the calendar.

3. Toggle through different calendar views by clicking the "Day," "Week," and "Month" buttons.

4. View a mini-calendar of the entire month. Use the double arrows at either side of the title to move to the previous or next month.

5. View and edit calendars you've already created and add or create new ones. (More instructions later!)

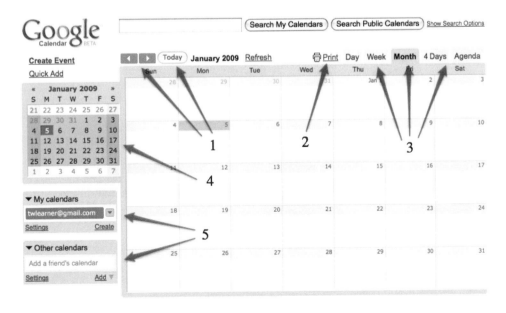

Adding Events

There are several ways to add events to your Google Calendar. Here are three options.

Option 1 – Click and Enter

1. Click the desired date "box" on the calendar. A pop-up window will appear.

2. Enter the event and time. Note – You can enter a phrase such as, "Technology Meeting in Room 414 at 4 pm." (Google Calendar is smart enough to recognize the time and location within your phrase!)

3. Click the "Create Event" button.

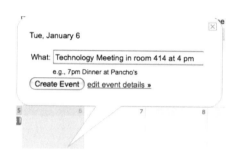

Option 2 – Use the Create Event link

1. Click the "Create Event" link in the upper-left corner of the screen.

2. Fill out the provided form, including the "What," "When," "Where," and "Description" fields.

3. Pull down the "repeats" menu to choose options for events that repeat every day, every week, or every month.

4. Click the "Save" button at the top of the window.

Option 3 – Use the Quick Add link

1. Click the "Quick Add" link in the upper-left corner of the screen.

2. Enter the event, day/date, and time. Note – You can enter a phrase such as, "Parent Open House on Sept. 15 at 7 pm" or "Volleyball game Friday at 8 pm."

   Google Calendar is smart enough to recognize the time and day/date within your phrase!

3. Press the enter key on your keyboard, or click the "+" button at the right side of the window.

Quick Tips for Google Calendars

To Edit an Event:

1. Click the desired event in your Google Calendar.

2. Make the desired changes.

3. Click the "Save" button at the top of the window.

To Delete an Event:

1. Click the desired event in your Google Calendar.

2. Click the "Delete" button at the top of the window.

To Set a Reminder for an event:

1. Click the desired event in your Google Calendar.

2. Locate the "Options" area at the right side of the window.

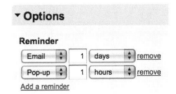

3. Use the pull-down menus and fields to get a reminder a certain number of minutes, hours, days, or weeks before the event.
   Note – An email reminder will send a message to the email address associated with your Google account. A pop-up reminder will appear in your browser.

To Move an Event:

In the calendar view, click and drag the event to the desired date.

Searching Your Calendar

1. Locate the search window at the top of the page.

2. Enter the desired keyword(s).

3. Click the "Search My Calendars" button.

4. This will return a list of events that include your keyword.

5. For advanced searches, click the "Show Search Options" link at the right side of the search buttons.

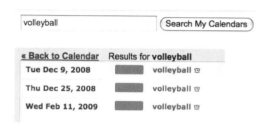

Renaming Calendars

1. Locate the desired calendar in the "My calendars" or "Other calendars" at the left side of the page.

2. Click the pull-down arrow beside the desired calendar title; pull down to "Calendar Settings."

3. Enter the desired calendar name.

4. Click the "Save" button.

Creating Additional Calendars

You may want to maintain separate calendars for your school events and your personal/family events:

1. Locate the "My calendars" area at the left side of the page.

2. Click the "Create" link.

3. Enter the name of your new calendar.

4. Click the "Create Calendar" button.

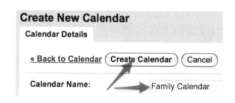

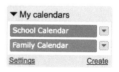

Adding Public Calendars

You can easily add calendars that have already been created.

1. Click the "Search Public Calendars" button at the top of the page.

2. Search or browse to find the desired calendar.

3. Click the "Add to Calendar" button.

4. Click the "Back to Calendar" link in the upper-left corner of the page.

5. Public calendars will be listed under "Other calendars" at the left side of the page.

Showing/Hiding Calendars

You can easily choose which calendar(s) you want to see in the calendar view.

1. Click the blank space beside a calendar title to toggle between the show/hide view.

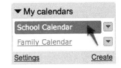

2. If the calendar title is highlighted, it is showing; if the calendar title is not highlighted, it is hidden.

Changing Calendar Colors

You can change each calendar to a different color so that you can easily distinguish them in your calendar view.

1. Click the pull-down triangle beside the calendar title.

2. Locate the color choices at the bottom of the pull-down window.

3. Click to select the desired color.

Deleting a Calendar

1. Click the "Settings" link in the "My calendars" area at the left side of the page.

2. Click the trashcan icon beside the calendar you wish to delete.

Sharing a Calendar

Need to do some collaborative scheduling of events? Why not create a shared calendar?

1. Click the pull-down triangle beside a calendar title and choose "Share this calendar."

2. Enter the email address of the person with whom you want to share your calendar.

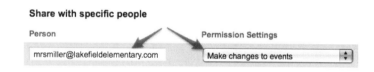

3. Pull down to choose the permission settings.

4. Click Save. This will generate an email message to the specified person will with instructions for viewing/hiding the shared calendar.

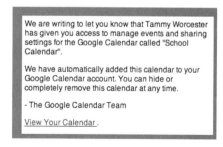

Google Calendar in iGoogle

You can view your Google Calendar in your iGoogle page!

1. Go to: www.google.com; Click the "iGoogle" link at the upper-right.

2. Add the "Google Calendar" gadget. (See page 19 for instructions.)

3. The Google Calendar gadget will show a mini-calendar at the top and a list of upcoming events at the bottom.

4. Click the "Add" link at the bottom of the gadget to add an event.

5. To hide/show calendars, click the "Options" link at the bottom and pull up to "Edit Visible Calendars"; click to select the desired calendar(s).

Embedding Your Google Calendar into a Blog or Web Page

1. Locate the "My calendars" area at the left side of the page.

2. Click the pull-down triangle beside the calendar title and pull down to "Calendar Settings."

3. Click the "Calendar Details" tab at the top of the settings window.

4. Scroll down to locate the "Embed This Calendar" area.

5. Click the provided link to customize the color, size, etc., and to choose which calendar(s) to include.

6. Copy the provided code and paste it into your web page or blog. (See page 48 for instructions.)

Google Calendar Ideas for Teachers

Lesson Plans

1. Create a calendar for each subject you teach (elementary) or for each class period (middle or high school).

2. Add an event for each subject for each day for the week.

    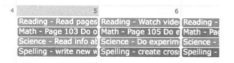

    a. In the "What" field, enter the subject name and a brief overview of the task for the day.

    b. In the "Description" field, enter details about the lesson plan, including any or all of the following:
        - objectives and standards
        - detailed teacher notes
        - equipment/resource lists
        - prerequisites
        - links to related websites

3. In the "Month" view, click an event to read the detailed description.

    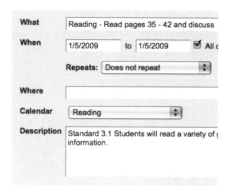

    Bonus! If you don't have time for a task on Friday, just click and drag it to Monday. No need to re-type it!

4. For a brief overview, switch to the "Agenda" view.

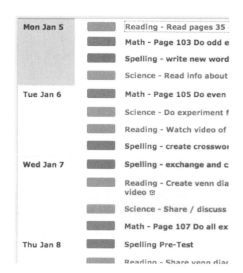

5. Embed your lesson plan calendar in your blog or webpage. (optional)

The image at the right shows the calendar embedded in a blog.
Size 400 x 500
View = Agenda

6. Add your calendar to your iGoogle page for easy access!

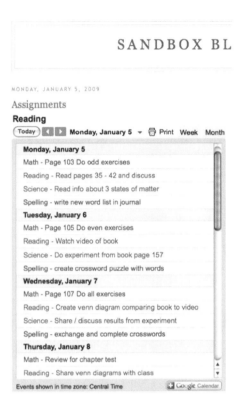

Coordinating family events

Create a calendar for each member of your immediate family to keep track of everyone's schedule.

- Print individual and family calendars each week.

- Create and share calendars to keep track of events from extended family members.

Planning a reunion or vacation

Create and share a calendar with others so that you can coordinate dates and events.

Google Calendar Ideas for Students
(Requires a Google Account)

Student Agendas

Students can set up a Google calendar to keep track of assignments, due dates, and personal information.

1. Create a calendar for different categories such as:
    - Assignments
    - Due Dates
    - Extracurricular
    - Personal

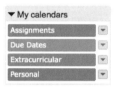

2. Add related events for each category to the calendar.

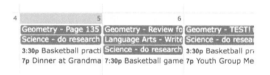

3. Use the description area to add detailed information about an event.

4. Students can add their Google Calendar to their iGoogle page for easy access!

Collaborative Project Organization

Students can use the shared calendar option to keep track of due dates, set goals, and track individual contributions to a group project.

Gmail

Gmail is Google's easy-to-use email system. Set up an additional email account in Gmail for personal use – or organize all of your email accounts in Gmail.

Author's note – I'm assuming you know the basics of how to compose and send email messages, so I'll use this section to showcase some of the unique features of Gmail.

Gmail

Getting Started

1. Go to: http://mail.google.com

2. Sign in using your Google Account.

   Note – If your Google login does not end in "@gmail.com" follow the on-screen prompts to set up your Gmail account.

Adding a Theme

1. Click the "settings" link in the upper-right corner of the screen.

2. Click the "Themes" link.

3. Click to choose the desired theme.

   Note – Some themes (such as Bus Stop) will ask you to enter your location. As you view your Gmail page, the theme will change to reflect the current time and/or weather conditions for your location.

Adding a Signature
Want your address and/or phone number to show at the bottom of messages you send? Add a signature.

1. Click the "settings" link in the upper-right corner of the screen.

2. Click the "General" link.

3. Scroll down to locate the "Signature" area.

4. Enter the desired information.

5. Scroll to the bottom and click the "Save Changes" button.

Consolidating Email Accounts

Tired of checking multiple email accounts?
Consolidate all of your accounts in Gmail!

1. Click the "settings" link in the upper-right corner of the screen.

2. Click the "Accounts" link.

3. In the "Get mail…" area, click the "Add another mail account" link.

4. Follow the on-screen prompts to:

   a. Enter the email address.
   (Example: This could be your school email address, a Yahoo mail address, or even another Gmail address.)

   b. Enter the password for your account.
   Click to "Leave a copy…" and to "Label incoming messages."
   Click the "Add Account" button.

   c. Click "Yes…" to be able to send mail from this account.

   d. Click the "Send Verification" button.
   Check your mail from the other account to verify!

5. Now you can read and answer email from your other account(s) right in Gmail! To show only the mail from that account, click the address in the "Labels" area at the left side of the page.

Quick Tips for Gmail

Creating Labels

Adding labels to messages allows you to easily sort and find them later.

1. Click the "settings" link in the upper-right corner.

2. Click the "Labels" tab.

3. Enter a label in the provided box; click the "Create" button. Repeat to create as many labels as you want. (You can always add more later!)

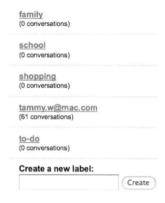

Applying Labels to Messages

For an individual email message:

1. Click the desired message to open it.

2. Pull down the "More Actions" menu and choose the desired label. Repeat to choose additional labels. (You can apply more than one label to each message!)

For multiple email messages:

1. In the inbox, click the check box in front of the desired messages.

2. Pull down the "More Actions" menu and choose the desired label. Repeat to choose additional labels. (You can apply more than one label to each message!)

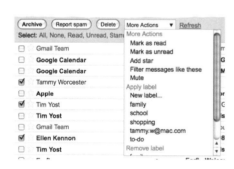

Finding "Labeled" Messages

1. Locate the "Labels" area at the left side of the page.

2. Click the desired label. Now only messages with that label will show.

    Note – If the Label is bold, that indicates that it contains unread messages.

3. Click the "Inbox" link at the left to show all messages again.

Applying Filters

You can automatically apply labels to messages with the use of filters.

1. Click the "settings" link in the upper-right corner of the screen.

2. Click the "Filters" tab.

3. Click the "Create a New Filter" link.

4. Enter the desired criteria in any or all of the provided fields; click the "Next Step" button.

5. Click the check box in front of "Apply the label" and choose the desired label from the pull-down menu.

6. Click the "Create Filter" button.

   Note – In the images at the above, I created a filter that will automatically apply the "shopping" label to all existing and incoming email messages from Coldwater Creek.

Starred Messages

Use the star icon to mark important messages.

1. In the inbox, click the star icon in front of your important messages.

2. To find all starred messages, click the "Starred" link at the left side of the screen.

Composing Messages

1. Click the "Compose Mail" link at the left side of the screen.

2. In the provided fields, enter the mail to address, the subject, and the message.

3. Use the provided editing toolbar to add emoticons and change fonts, styles, sizes, etc.

Searching Messages

1. Enter the desired keyword(s) in the search window at the top of the page.

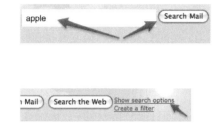

2. Click the "Search Mail" button.

3. For advanced search options, click the "Show search options" link.

4. Use the advanced search fields to do a more detailed search of messages.

Gmail in iGoogle

You can easily access and manage your email messages right in your iGoogle page!

1. Go to: www.google.com; click the "iGoogle" link at the upper-right.

2. Add the "Gmail" gadget. (See page 19 for instructions.)

3. The Gmail gadget will show a list of messages in your inbox.

4. Click the maximize icon at the upper-right corner of the window to open your Gmail gadget in a full-page view.

5. In the full-page gadget window you can reply to messages, compose messages, and even add labels!

Adding Gmail Contacts

To manually add contacts:

1. Click the "Contacts" link at the left side of the page.

2. Click the "New Contact" button at the upper-left corner of the contacts window.

3. Enter the desired information in the provided fields; click "Save."

To add contacts from an existing email message:

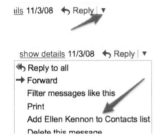

1. Open the desired message.

2. Click the triangle beside the "Reply" link.

3. From the pull-down menu, choose to "Add _____ to Contacts list."

Creating Contact Groups

1. Click the "Contacts" link at the left side of the page.

2. Click the "New Group" button at the top-left corner of the contacts window.

3. Enter a name for your new group.

4. Repeat steps 2 and 3 for each group you want to add.

5. Add group members:

   a. Click to select the names of the desired contacts.

   b. Pull down the "Groups" button to select the desired group.

6. To send a message to everyone in the group:

   a. Click the "Compose Mail" link at the upper-left corner of the screen.

   b. In the "To" field, enter the group name. This will enter the email addresses of ALL members of the group!

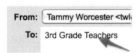

Google Sites

Google sites offers a way to create your own individual website or group "wiki." There's no need to worry about designing an attractive layout or finding server space for your pages – Google Sites does that for you!

Google Sites

Getting Started

1. Go to: http://sites.google.com

2. Sign in using your Google Account.

Creating a Site

1. Click the "Create Site" button.

2. Follow the on-screen prompts and fill in the fields to create your site.

   Note – You can create as many sites as you want in the future. For now, let's just set up a practice (or sandbox) site.

   a. Enter the site name, "Your Initials Sandbox Site."

   b. Note the URL of your site. My address (URL) will be: http://sites.google.com/site/twsandboxsite

   c. Enter a description (optional).

   d. Click to choose the sharing options. (You can easily change this later.)

   e. Choose a theme.

   f. Enter the verification code.

   g. Click the "Create site" button!

Editing the Home Page

The first page (the home page) of your site has already been created for you. Let's use this as our welcome page.

1. Click the "Edit page" button at the top-left corner of the page.

2. Change the title and enter a brief welcome message.

3. Click the "Save" button.

Creating Additional Pages

1. Click the "Create new page" button at the top-left corner.

2. Enter a title for your new page.

3. Select the desired type of page.

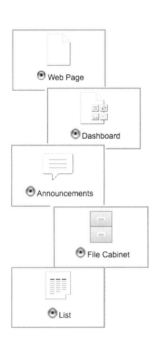

   a. **Web Page** – A web page is sort of like a word processing document. You can add and edit text, and embed tables, hyperlinks, images, and more!

   b. **Dashboard** – A dashboard includes a two-column layout with spaces that hold gadgets.

   c. **Announcement** – An announce page is a place to post chronological information such as news, project updates, or announcements.

   d. **File Cabinet** – A file cabinet page allows you to store and manage documents from your hard drive.

   e. **List** – A list page lets you easily keep and manage lists – school supplies needed, to-do lists, assignments, lists of websites, etc.

4. Choose the location for your new page. (See more about page hierarchy on the following page.)

5. Click the "Create Page" button.

Page Hierarchy

In the "Create New Page" area, you'll be asked where you want to put the page. (See image at right)

For this sandbox site, we'll just put all of the pages at the top level. However, for future sites, you might want a more complex hierarchy.

It might help to think about your site like an outline. A classroom website might look something like this:

> Welcome Page (*Home Page*)
> Classroom News (*Announcement*)
> Daily Assignments (*Web Page*)
> > Geometry (*List or Announcement*)
> > Algebra (*List or Announcement*)
> > Calculus (*List or Announcement*)
> Forms & Documents (*File Cabinet*)
> Web Resources (*Web Page*)
> > Geometry (*List*)
> > Algebra (*List*)
> > Calculus (*List*)
> Helpful Tools (*Dashboard*)

Web Page Basics

1. Follow the instructions on page 100 to create a new web page. (For your sandbox site, create an "About the Author" page.)

2. Click the "Edit page" button in the upper-left corner of the screen.

3. Enter a paragraph or two about yourself.

4. Use the editing toolbar to change fonts, sizes, styles, etc.

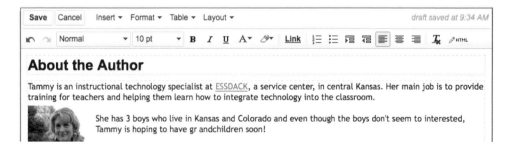

Web Page Options

Adding an Image

1. Pull down the "Insert" menu to "Image."

2. Follow the on-screen prompts to upload an image from your hard drive or to add one from a web address (URL).

3. Click the picture and use the pop-up menu bar to change the alignment, size, and wrapping options.

Tammy is an instructional technology specialist at for teachers and helping them learn how to integr

She has 3 boys who live in Kansa hoping to have grandchildren so

Align: L C R - Size: S M L Original - Wrap: **on**

Adding a Hyperlink

1. Select the text that you want to become the link.

2. Click the "Link" button in the editing toolbar.

ialist at ESSDACK, a service o integrate technology into

3. Follow the on-screen prompts to link to an existing page (another page in your Google site) or to a web address (URL).

Adding a Table

1. Pull down the "Table" menu to "Insert Table."

2. Pull over to choose the desired table size.

Contact Information:

Phone	839-495-3849
Cell	934-534-0382
Email	twemail@gmail.com

3. Select a cell and then click and drag the edge to resize it.

4. Use the options in the "Table" menu to insert or delete rows and columns.

Adding Columns

1. Pull down the "layout" menu to change to a two-column layout.

2. Enter information, images, and tables in both columns. Note – Columns will expand downward when information is added. Information will not wrap from the first column in to the second.

t ESSDACK, a
to provide
to integrate

ias and
boys don't seem
to have

Contact Information:

Phone	839-495-3849
Cell	934-534-0382
Email	twemail@gmail.com

Dashboard Page Basics

1. Follow the instructions on page 100 to create a new dashboard page.

2. Click the "Edit page" link at the top of the screen.

3. Click one of the provided gadget "boxes" and choose a gadget from the pop-up menu.

4. Repeat step 3 for additional gadgets.
   Note – If you want more than 4 gadgets, you can add more by using the "Insert" menu.

5. Add text above and/or below each gadget if you want.

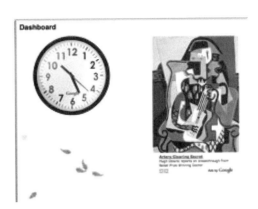

Announcements Page Basics

1. Follow the instructions on page 100 to create a new announcements page.

2. Click the "New Post" button.

3. Enter the desired title and message. Change fonts, sizes, and styles, if desired.

4. Click the "Save" button.

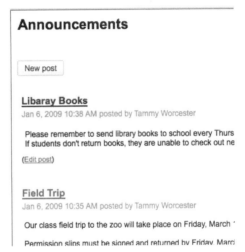

File Cabinet Page Basics

Use the file cabinet to organize files that parents and/or students can download.

1. Follow the instructions on page 100 to create a new file cabinet page.

2. Click the "Add file" button to choose and upload files.

3. Use the "Move to" button to create folders and move files into folders.

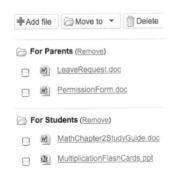

List Page Basics

You can create a variety of different types of lists. For our sandbox blog, let's create a list of web resources.

1. Follow the instructions on page 100 to create a new list page.

2. Click the "Create a Custom List" button.

3. Follow the on-screen prompts to create the following columns:
   Title – text type
   Address – URL type
   Comments – text type

4. Click the "Add item" button to add the desired web resources.

Site Navigation

You can include the pages you've created in the navigation menu at the upper-left side of the screen.

1. Use the "Sitemap" link to move to one of your pages.

2. Pull down the "More actions" button to "Page Settings."

3. Click to "Show this in "Navigation…"

4. Click "Save."

5. Repeat steps 1-4 to add each of your pages to the navigation menu.

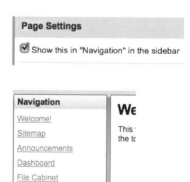

Editing the Sidebar

1. Click the "Edit sidebar" link at the bottom-left corner of the screen.

2. Follow the on-screen prompts to add or delete sidebar items.

3. To change the order of items in the navigation menu:

    a. Click the "edit" link in the Navigation area.

    b. Use the arrows to move items up or down in the navigation menu.

    c. Use the "X" button to delete items from the navigation menu.

    d. Click "Save" and then click the "Return to Site" link in the upper-left corner.

Customizing the Site Appearance

1. Pull down the "Site Settings" button to "Change Appearance."

2. Click the "Site Elements" tab and follow the on-screen prompts to change the site layout, add a header logo, and edit the sidebar.

3. Click the "Colors and Fonts" tab and follow the on-screen prompts to change background colors and text colors.

4. Click the "Themes" tab and click to select a new theme for your site.

5. Click the "Save Changes" button.

6. To exit the settings window, click the "Return to site" link in the upper-left corner.

Sharing Your Site

You can invite others to view and/or edit your site.

1. Pull down the "Site Settings" button to "Share this site."

2. Enter the desired email address (or addresses).

3. Click to choose the desired level of permissions:

   a. **Owners**

      An owner has the same permissions as the site creator. Owners can add and edit pages, change colors and layouts, invite others, and even delete the site.

   b. **Collaborators**

      A collaborator can add, edit, and delete pages, and add pages to the navigation menu.

   c. **Viewers**

      A viewer can only view pages.

4. Click the "Invite these people" button.

Reviewing Changes

Google Sites keeps a history of changes.

1. Click the "See earlier versions" link in the upper-right corner of the screen.

2. Click the version title link to view a previous version.

3. Click the link at the right to revert to a previous version.

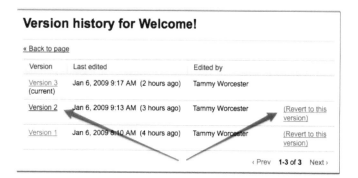

4. Click the "home" link at the bottom of the page to return to the site.

Google Docs

Google Docs allows you to create and share word processing files, spreadsheets, and presentations. Since the documents are stored online, you can access and edit them from any computer with an Internet connection!

In this section, we'll explore the three main areas of Google Docs:

- **Document** – a document is a word processor similar to Microsoft Word or Pages.

- **Presentation** – a presentation is a slide-show program similar to PowerPoint or Keynote.

- **Spreadsheet** – a spreadsheet is a program similar to Excel or Numbers.

Google Docs

Getting Started

1. Go to: http://docs.google.com

2. Sign in using your Google Account.

Google Documents Basics

1. Pull down the "New" menu to "Document."

2. Click the "Untitled" text at the top-left corner to change the title of the page.

3. Enter the desired text in the "body" area.

4. Use the editing toolbar at the top to change fonts, sizes, styles, alignments, etc.

5. Click the "Save" button in the upper-right corner.

The Page View

1. Pull down the "View" menu to switch between the normal view and the fixed-width page view.

2. Pull down the "View" menu to view the document in full-screen mode.

   Press the escape key on your keyboard to return to the normal view.

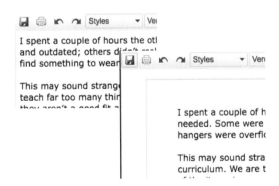

Adding an Image

1. Pull down the "Insert" menu to "Picture."

2. Follow the on-screen prompts to upload an image from your hard drive or to add one from a web address (URL).

3. Use the options at the bottom of the window to change the size, alignment, and wrapping options for the picture.

I spent a c
more cloth
others did
overflowin
morning.

This may s
representa
too many things. And, like my article
and outdated, or they aren't a good f

Adding a Table

1. Pull down the "Table" menu to "Insert Table."

2. Pull over to choose the desired table size.

3. Select a cell and then click and drag the edge to resize it.

4. Use the options in the "Table" menu to insert or delete rows and columns.

Contact Information:

Phone	839-495-3849
Cell	934-534-0382
Email	twemail@gmail.com

Adding a Link

1. Select the text that you want to become the link.

2. Click the "Link" button in the editing toolbar.

3. Follow the on-screen prompts to link to:

   a. **URL** – Link to an external web page.

   b. **Document** – Link to another document created in Google Docs.

   c. **Bookmark** – Link to a specified location within this document. (Pull down the "Insert" menu to set a bookmark; then link to it.)

   d. **Email** – Link to your email address.

but I think my closet is
iools' curriculum. We ar
iany of the items in our

Insert Link

Link To

⦿ URL   ○ Document   ○ Bookmark

URL: |

Link Display

Text:

The hyper-linked text, like Click me for the best lo

Footnotes

1. Pull down the "View" menu and make sure the "Footnotes" option is checked.

2. Click to insert the cursor where you wish to insert a footnote.

3. Pull down the "Insert" menu to footnote.

4. Enter the footnote information in the provided area at the right side of the page.
   Note – This can be entered as a simple URL or in proper bibliographical format such as MLA or APA.

5. To delete a footnote, click the pull down triangle in the right corner and choose "Delete."

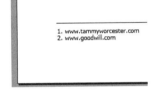

6. When you print, the footnotes will be listed at the bottom of each page.

Writing Tools

1. Pull down the "Tools" menu to access the following:

   a. **Check Spelling**
      Checks spelling of all words in the document. Misspelled words will be highlighted. Click a highlighted word to choose from a list of suggested spellings.

   b. **Word Count**
      The word count option provides a count of words, characters, paragraphs, sentences, and pages, along with readability statistics.

   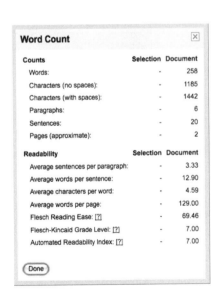

   c. **Look Up Word**
      Will provide a definition, synonyms, and maybe even an encyclopedia entry for the selected word.

   d. **Search the Web for Word**
      Will do a "Google search" for web pages or images related to the selected word.

Printing Your Document

Option 1 – Print as PDF file.

1. Pull down the "File" menu to "Print."

2. Follow the on-screen prompts to save, open, and print the file with Adobe Reader (or another PDF reader.)

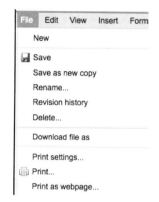

Option 2 – Print as Web Page

1. Pull down the "File" menu to "Print as webpage." (The document will open in a new browser window.)

2. Use your browser's print options to print the page.

Sharing Your Document

Option 1 - Invite others to view and/or edit your document.

1. Pull down the "Share" button to "Share with others."

2. Enter the desired email address (or addresses).

3. Click to choose the desired level of permissions:

   a. **Collaborators** – A collaborator can add, edit, and delete information. Note – up to 10 people can edit a document at the same time.

   b. **Viewers –** A viewer can only view pages.

4. Click the "Invite collaborators" button.

Option 2 - Publish your document for anyone to view.

1. Pull down the "Share" tab in the upper-right corner to "Publish as web page."

2. Click the "Publish document" button.

3. Click to choose whether you want the page to automatically re-publish when changes are made.

4. Return to this area at any time to "stop publishing."

Inserting Comments

This is extremely helpful when collaborating with others on a document.

1. Click to insert the cursor where you want the comment to appear.

2. Pull down the "Insert" menu to "Comment."

3. Enter the desired comment. (Notice it will show who made the comment and when it was made.)

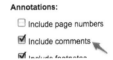

4. Click the highlighted comment to change the color or to delete it.

5. Pull down the "File" menu to "Print Settings" to determine whether or not you want the comments to print.

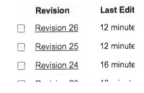

Reviewing Changes

1. Pull down the "Tools" menu to "Revision History." You'll see a list of revisions, with the most recent at the top.

2. Click a revision title to view it.

3. Use the buttons at the top of the page to view older or newer revisions, publish this revision, or revert to this revision.

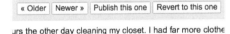

4. Click the "Back to…" links in the upper left corner to return to the document.

Classroom Ideas/Activities for Google Documents

The Teacher can:

- Create and share a document with other teachers to collaborate on a lesson plan or project.

- Collaborate with other teachers to track the status and record notes and observations about a special needs student you share.

- Use Google Docs to easily access the same document(s) from your home computer and your school computer.

For Students

If students have a Google account, they can create and share their own documents.

The student can:

- Share a document with the teacher, allowing the teacher to check their progress and/or edit their work.

- Share with each other to peer-edit their writing.

- Write a collaborative story.

- Take class notes and then share them with others.

- Create documents at school and then access and edit them at home.

- Collaborate with students from a different school, city, state, or country!

- Share ideas while planning a group project.

Google Presentation

Creating Slides with Text

1. From the Docs Home page, pull down the "New" menu to "Presentation."

2. Click the "Untitled" text in the top-left corner to change the title of the page.

3. Enter the desired text on the slide.

4. Use the editing menu at the top of the page to change fonts, sizes, styles, etc. as desired and to add bullet points.

5. Pull down the "Slide" menu to "New slide," or click the "+" button in the upper-left corner of the page.

6. Choose the desired slide layout for the new slide.

7. Repeat steps 3-5 to build a slide show.

Adding a Slide Design

Option 1 – Themes:

1. Pull down the "Edit" menu to "Change Theme."

2. Click to choose the desired design.
   (The theme will be applied to all slides in your presentation.)

3. To remove a theme, pull down the "Edit" menu to "Change Theme," and choose "blank."

Option 2 – Backgrounds

1. Pull down the "Edit" menu to "Change Background."

2. Use the on-screen prompts to choose a color or to upload an image from your hard drive.

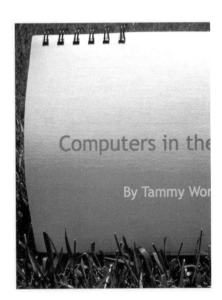

Adding Shapes

1. Pull down the "Insert" menu to "Shapes" and pull over to choose the desired shape.

2. Click and drag the shape in the center to move it; click and drag a corner to resize it.

3. Use the "Fill Color" tool to change the color of the shape.

4. To add text to the shape, pull down the "Insert" menu to "Text." Type the desired text and then move the text box over the shape.

Adding Images

1. Pull down the "Insert" menu to "Image" or click the "image" button at the top of the window.

2. Follow the on-screen prompts to upload an image from your computer or add an image from a website URL.

3. Click and drag the picture in the center to move it; click and drag a corner to resize it.

Adding Videos

1. Pull down the "Insert" menu to "Video."

2. Use the provided search window to find a YouTube video.

3. Click to select the desired video.

4. Click the "Insert Video" button.

5. Move the video to the desired location on the slide.

6. Use the controls at the bottom of the video to start/stop play, adjust the volume, and show in full-screen mode.

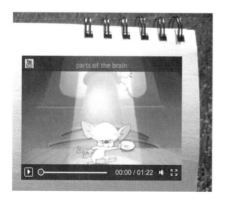

Viewing Slides/Changing Order

1. Locate the mini-slides at the left side of the screen.

2. Click a slide to view it.

3. Click and drag a slide to move it to a new position.

Adding Speaker Notes

1. Click the "View Speaker Notes" in the bottom-right corner of the slide.

2. At the right side of the slide, add notes for each slide.

3. Click the "x" button in the upper-right corner to hide the speaker notes.

Presenting the Slide Show

1. Click the "Start presentation" button in the upper-right corner of the screen.

2. To advance the slides use one of these methods:
   - Press the space bar on your keyboard.
   - Press the enter key on your keyboard.
   - Use the arrow keys on your keyboard.
   - Click the mouse button.
   - Use the icon(s) in the lower-left corner of the slide.

3. To view speaker notes, click the "View Speaker Notes" in the upper-right corner of the page.

4. To quit the slide show, press the "Escape" key on your keyboard.

Sharing Via Invitation
Invite others to view and/or edit your presentation.

1. Pull down the "Share" button to "Share with others."

2. Enter the desired email address (or addresses).

3. Click to choose the desired level of permissions:

   a. **Collaborators** – A collaborator can add, edit, and delete information. Note – up to 10 people can edit a presentation at the same time.

   b. **Viewers –** A viewer can only view pages.

4. Click the "Invite collaborators" button.

Sharing Via Publishing
A quick way to share your presentation is to publish it and then share the URL.

1. Pull down the "Share" button to "Publish/Embed."

2. Click the "Start Publishing" button.

3. Share the provided URL with your desired audience. (See page 139 for tips for sharing a long URL.)

Shared-Presentation Options

• After receiving their invitation, collaborators and viewers can all view the slide show at the same time!

• Individuals can click through the slides at their own pace, or a member of the group can take control of the slide show by clicking the "Take control…" link in the upper-right corner.

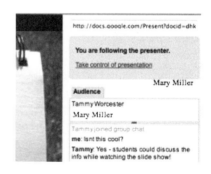

• Members can chat, using the window at the right side of the screen. Enter the desired message in the text box at the bottom of the screen and press the "enter" key on your keyboard.

• Only 10 members can *edit* the presentation at the same time; however, up to 200 people can *view* it!

Reviewing Changes

1. Pull down the "Tools" menu to "Revision History." You'll see a list of revisions, with the most recent at the top.

2. Click a revision title to view it. (It will open in a new tab or a new window.)

3. Use the button at the top of the page to revert to this revision or close the tab/window to return to the list.

4. Click the "Back to editor" link in the upper-left corner to return to the document.

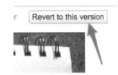

Embedding Your Presentation

You can easily embed your presentation into a blog or website!

1. Pull down the "Share" button to "Publish/Embed."

2. Click the "Start Publishing" button.

3. Use the pull-down menu to select the desired presentation size.

4. Copy the provided code; paste it into a blog entry or a web page.

Printing Your Presentation

1. Pull down the "File" menu to "Print."

2. Use the options at the right side of the print window to choose a layout and show or hide the background and speaker notes.

3. Click the buttons at the bottom of the print window to "Print" or "Save as PDF."

Classroom Ideas/Activities for Google Presentations

Note – Many of the PowerPoint activities in Tammy's "50 Quick & Easy" books can be done using Google Presentations tool.

The teacher can:

- Create presentations to introduce or review new concepts.

- Work on the same presentation both at home and at school.

- Allow students (with Google Accounts) to have a backchannel chat while following a presentation.

- Collaborate with other teachers to create a group presentation.

- Collaborate with students to create a whole-class presentation. (The teacher creates a slide for each student. Students then edit their own slide.)

- Create a photo slide show and embed it in his/her blog.

The student can:

- Create a presentation for any content area.

- Share a presentation with the teacher, allowing the teacher to check their progress and/or edit their work.

- Create presentations at school and then access and edit them at home.

- Collaborate with students from a different school, city, state, or country!

- Share a presentation with a parent or grandparent.

Google Spreadsheet

Google Spreadsheet is loaded with fabulous tools and features. In this book, we'll just cover the basics. To gain more advanced skills, use the "Help" menu to find online tutorials.

Getting Started

1. From the Docs Home page, pull down the "New" menu to "Spreadsheet."

2. Click the "Unsaved Spreadsheet" link in the upper-left corner to rename the file.

3. Enter text in the desired cells. Use the "edit" menu at the top of the screen to change fonts, sizes, styles, etc.

Resizing Columns

1. Move your mouse into the header area. (The header area is where you see the A, B, C labels.)

2. Click and drag the line between two columns. Drag to the right to make the column larger; drag to the left to make it smaller.

   or

   Double-click the line between two columns. The column will automatically shrink or expand to fit the data.

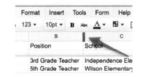

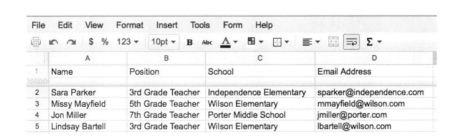

Creating a Chart/Graph

1. Enter the desired data.

2. Click and drag to select the cells with data.

3. Pull down the "Insert" menu to "Chart."

4. In the "Create chart" window:

    a. Choose the chart type.

    b. Add Labels.

    c. Group the data by rows or columns.

    d. Use rows and/or columns as labels.

    e. See a preview of your chart.

5. Click the "Save Chart" button.

6. Click and drag the top of the chart to move it.

7. Click and drag a corner of the chart to resize it.

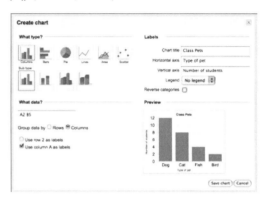

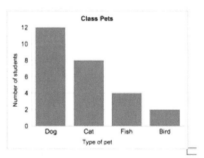

Basic Functions

1. Enter 10 numbers in each column A, B, and C.

2. Click in cell A11.

3. Pull down the "Formula" button to "sum."

4. Click and drag to select cells A1 through A10.

5. Press the enter key on your keyboard.

6. Using what you learned in steps 2-5, repeat the procedure to calculate the *average* of the numbers in column B.

7. Then use your skills to calculate the *maximum* of the numbers in column C.

Sharing/Collaboration Options

Important – Google Spreadsheets allows users to edit a spreadsheet without signing in. That means your students can collaborate on a spreadsheet file you create – even if they don't have a Google account!

Sharing Via Invitation
Invite others to view and/or edit your spreadsheet.

1. Pull down the "Share" button to "Invite People."

2. Enter the desired email address (or addresses), subject, and message.

3. Click to choose the desired level of permissions and privacy.

   a. **To Edit** – A collaborator can add, edit, and delete information. (Up to 50 people can edit a spreadsheet at the same time.)

   b. **To View –** A viewer can only view the spreadsheet. (Up to 200 people can view a spreadsheet at the same time.)

4. Click the "Send" button.

Sharing With the World
A quick way to share your spreadsheet is to use this option.

1. Pull down the "Share" menu to "Share with the World."

2. Choose the desired privacy option.

3. Share the provided URL with the desired people. (See page 139 for tips for sharing a long URL.)

4. Click the "Save" button. (Viewers will not be able to access the spreadsheet until you have clicked this button!)

Publishing the Spreadsheet

If you want others to view, but not edit the spreadsheet, do this:

1. Pull down the "Share" button to "Publish as Web Page."

2. Click the "Publish now" button.

3. Share the provided URL with your desired audience. (See page 139 for tips for sharing a long URL.)

Reviewing Changes

1. Pull down the "Tools" menu to "Revision History."

2. Use the buttons at the top of the screen to view older and newer versions.

3. If you want to revert to a previous version, click the "Revert to this one" button.

4. If you want to return to the original document, click the "Back to editing" button.

Printing

To print the spreadsheet file:

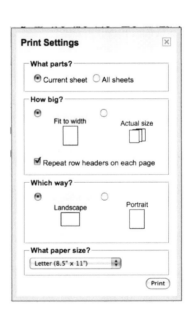

1. Pull down the "File" menu to "Print."

2. Click to choose:

   a. What parts you want to print.

   b. The size.

   c. The orientation.

   d. Your paper size.

3. Click the "Print" button.

Google Forms

Want an easy way to collect data for your spreadsheet? Use a form! Create a form; have others fill it out; and the data is automatically entered into a Google spreadsheet!

Creating a Google Form

1. From the Docs Home page, pull down the "New" menu to "Form."

2. Replace "Untitled form" with the desired title.

3. Enter some instructions for the end-user. (Optional)

4. Use the "Add question" button at the top of the window to add questions of different types: text, paragraph, multiple choice, check boxes, etc.

5. Use the buttons at the right side of each question to edit, duplicate, or delete the question.

6. Click the "Save" button.

Sharing the Form

Option 1 – Share the URL

1. Look at the very bottom of the screen to see the URL of the published form.

2. Share the URL with others.

Option 2 – Email the URL

1. Click the "Email Form" button at the top of the page.

2. Enter the desired email addresses and click "Send."

Option 3 – Embed the form in a blog or webpage

1. Click the "More Actions" button at the top of the page.

2. Copy the provide code and paste it into your blog or webpage.

Viewing Responses/Data

In the spreadsheet:

1. From the form-editing view, pull down the "See responses" button to "Spreadsheet."

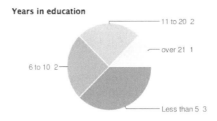

In the summary report view

1. From the form-editing view, pull down the "See responses" button to "Summary."

or

2. From the spreadsheet, pull down the "Form" menu to "Show Summary."

Navigating the Form and Spreadsheet

You can easily switch back and forth between the form-editing view, the live form, and the spreadsheet.

To open the spreadsheet:

1. From the form editor, pull down the "See responses" button to "Spreadsheet."

2. From the Docs home, click the spreadsheet title.

To open the form editor:

1. From the spreadsheet, pull down the "Form" menu to "Edit Form."

To open the live form:

1. From the spreadsheet, pull down the "Form" menu to "Go to Live Form."

or

2. From the form editor, click the link at the bottom of the screen.

Classroom Ideas/Activities for Google Spreadsheet

Note – Many of the PowerPoint activities in Tammy's "50 Quick & Easy" books can be done using Google Spreadsheet.

The Teacher can use a *spreadsheet* to:

- Keep track of attendance. (Student names in column A; dates across the top…)

- Create class checklists. (Student names in column A; whatever you want across the top.)

- Chart student progress.

- Calculate student grades.

- Create an electronic lesson plan book. (Days of the week in column A; subjects across the top.)

- Design and print rubrics.

The Teacher can use a *form* to:

- Collect information from students, parents, or teachers.

The Students can use a spreadsheet/form to:

- Gather data for research projects.

- Create charts and graphs of data.

- Perform calculations.

- Keep track of grades.

Organizing Google Docs Home

When you have created a number of Google documents, presentations, and spreadsheets, you may want to organize them into folders.

Creating Folders

1. Go to: http:/docs.google.com

2. Pull down the "New" menu to "Folder."

3. Enter the desired name for the folder.

4. Click the "Save" button.

5. Repeat steps 2-4 to create additional folders.
    (The folders will appear at the left side of the screen.)

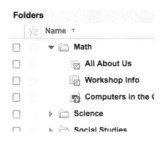

Putting Files into Folders

1. Click "All items" in the top-left corner.

2. Click and drag each file to the desired folder. Note – You can drag a file into more than one folder if you want.

Viewing Folder Contents

1. Click a folder at the left and view the contents in the main window.

    or

2. Click the "All folders" link at the left and in the main window, click the triangle icons to open and close folders.

Google Docs Templates

There's no reason to create all of your Google Docs files from scratch. Google has lots of great templates that can save you tons of time!

Viewing the Templates

1. From the Google Documents home page (docs.google.com), pull down the "New" menu to "From Template…"

   or

2. Go to: http://docs.google.com/templates

3. Use the categories at the left to browse the templates and use the search window at the top to search for a particular template.
   (Be sure to check out the templates for students and teachers!)

4. Click the tabs at the top to sort by file type.

Using a Template

1. Click the "Use this template" button.

2. When the file opens, click the title in the upper-left corner and change it.

3. The file will save automatically to your Google Docs home page.

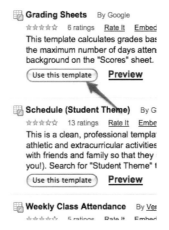

Gmail in iGoogle

You can easily access and manage your email messages right in your iGoogle page!

1. Go to: www.google.com; click the "iGoogle" link at the upper-right.

2. Add the "Google Docs" gadget. (See page 19 for instructions.)

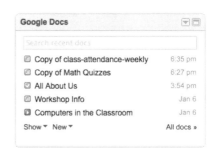

3. The Gmail gadget will show a list of messages in your inbox.

4. Click the maximize icon at the upper-right corner of the window to open your Gmail gadget in a full-page view.

5. In the full-page gadget window, you can reply to messages, compose messages, and even add labels!

Appendix

Appendix I
Google Accounts

In order to take advantage of many of Google's resources, you will need to have an account. In this section, you'll learn how to create accounts for both the teacher and the students.

Creating a Google Account for the Teacher

To create a teacher account, you can use either of these two options:

Option 1
Use an existing email address

1. Go to: www.google.com

2. Click the "Sign In" link in the upper-right corner.

3. Click the "Create an account now" link at the lower-right.

4. Follow the on-screen prompts to create an account.

   Note – The hardest part will most likely be the word verification where you will have to decipher a group of letters. Don't get discouraged if you can't get it right. It may take several tries...

5. Check your email for a message from Google. It will include a link that will verify and enable your account.

Option 2
Create a Gmail account

Note – once your Gmail account is created, you can use your Gmail address and password to log on to Google's other tools!

1. Go to: mail.google.com

2. Click the "Sign up for Gmail" link at the lower-right.

3. Follow the on-screen prompts to create your account.

Google Accounts for Students

As you already know, many (but not all) of Google's tools require an account. Students will need to sign in to a Google Account to do many of the activities in this book. So – what's the best option for student logins?

At this point, there is not a single best answer for everyone. Let's look at some options and consider the pros and cons of each.

Note – Be sure to check your school's acceptable use policy before setting up student accounts.

Option 1
Single Generic Student Login

As a teacher, you can create a second account for student use. All students will log in with the same name and password to access Google's tools. *If you are a non-techie and you work with students who don't have their own email accounts, this is probably your best option.*

Pros:
+ easy to set up
+ access to all Google tools and apps

Cons:
- no individual accountability

How to do it:

1. Go to: mail.google.com

2. Click the "Sign Up for Gmail" link at the lower-right.

3. Follow the on-screen prompts to create a student account.

    Think carefully about the login name and password. Remember, your students will use this information to log in. Let's say you are a 5th grade teacher at Anywhere Elementary School. You might want to use something like "AESStudent5" for the login and "AESstudentsrock!" for the password:

4. Now when your students are using a Google tool that requires a login, they can each sign in using the "AESStudent5@gmail.com" login and the "AESstudentsrock!" password.

Get started with Gmail

First name:	Anywhere
Last name:	Student
Desired Login Name:	AESstudent5
	Examples: JSmith, Johr
	check availability!
Choose a password:	AESstudentsrock!
	Minimum of 8 characters

Option 2
Student-Created Accounts

If your students have their own email addresses and/or if you work with students over 13, this is probably the best option for you.

For students who have their own email accounts:
If students already have an email account, they can set up their own Google account using Option 1 on page 133.

For students* who don't have email accounts:
Students can set up their own Google accounts using Option 2 on page 133.

* If students are 13 or younger, you should first get permission from parents or guardians.

Pros:
+ Access to all Google tools and apps
+ Individual logins/individual accountability

Cons:
+ No teacher control over accounts/passwords

Option 3
Student Accounts via Teacher Domain

If you are a high-end computer user or if you have a techie friend who can help, this is a great option. In this option, you will buy a domain name for your classroom and will use a "catchall" email address to create student accounts.

The directions on the next two pages will show you how to set up a domain and create student accounts.

Pros:
+ Access to all Google tools and apps
+ Individual logins/individual accountability
+ Teacher can reset lost passwords.

Cons:
- Requires a domain name which will cost anywhere from $1 – $15 per year.
- Requires some technical skill

Setting up the Domain

1. Go to www.GoDaddy.com (or another domain service) and purchase a domain name.

   a. The domain name should be short, but easy to remember. Try something similar to TWclass.info or MrsW.org.

   b. GoDaddy will try to entice you to purchase all sorts services. Do **not** buy any additional services. You **only** need to purchase the domain name! (My total bill for twclass.info was $1.21 for a year!)

2. In GoDaddy, go into the Email Management area for your domain:

   a. In the Forward Address window, enter "info" and your domain name.

   b. In the "Forward Mail to:" window, enter the email address you use at school. *It may take a couple of hours after the initial setup for the email forwarding to take effect.*

   c. Click to turn on the "Make Catchall Account" option.

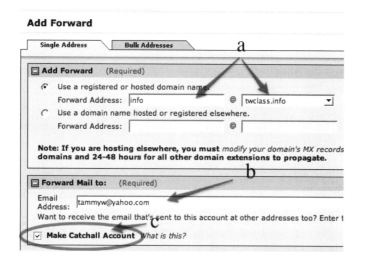

Now any email addressed to your domain name will be forwarded to your school email address. And you can put anything in front of the @ and it will still work. In the screen shot example above, it doesn't matter if the email is addressed to info@twclass.info or test@twclass.info or studentname@twclass.info, the message will be forwarded to my Yahoo account.

Creating Student Accounts

Once your catchall email address is created, *students* can use the following instructions to create their accounts. (Or the *teacher* can follow and repeat the instructions to create an account for each student.)

1. Go to: www.google.com

2. Click the "Sign In" link in the upper-right corner.

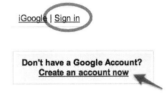

3. Click the "Create an account now" link at the lower-right.

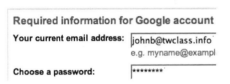

4. Follow the on-screen prompts to create an account.

   a. For the email address, the student will use studentname@yourdomain. Example: johnb@twclass.info

   b. The students can set their own password.

   Note – The hardest part will most likely be the word verification where you will have to decipher a group of letters. Don't get discouraged if you can't get it right. It may take several tries...

5. The *teacher* will receive an email and will need to verify the account for each student.

6. If a student forgets his/her password, click the "I cannot access my account" link. Follow the prompts for password recovery and enter the login email address (johnb@twclass.info). An email will be sent to the teacher and will allow the teacher to reset the password.

Option 4
Google Apps Editions
This option is the most secure, but it has some limitations.

There are 3 types of free Google Apps Editions:

Google Apps Team Edition
http://www.google.com/apps/edu/
If students have a school-issued (or teacher-issued) email address that contains the school's (or teacher's) domain (example: joestudent@USD356.com or joestudent@TWClass.info), they can create an account and automatically collaborate with others with the same email domain.

Users will go to: www.google.com/a/yourdomainhere
For access to: Google Sites, Docs, Calendar, and Chat.

Google Apps Standard Edition
http://www.google.com/a/cpanel/domain/new
Using your own domain name, you easily create up to 200 student accounts from a spreadsheet file. (If you don't already have a domain name, you can buy one for less than $10 a year.

Users will go to: www.google.com/a/yourdomainhere
For access to: Start Page, Calendar, Docs, Email, and Sites

Google Apps Education Edition
www.google.com/a/edu
Similar to Standard Edition but managed as a whole-school domain. Note – This option requires setup and management by a school IT person.

Users will go to: http://partnerpage.google.com/yourdomainhere
For access to: Gmail, Google Talk, Calendar, Docs, and Sites.

Pros:
+ Students have individual accounts; can track
  individual "posts"

Cons:
- Limited to certain apps (Google Maps, Google
  Notebook, and Google Reader, for example, are not
  included.)

Appendix II
Sharing a Long URL

As you create customized resources using Google's tools, you will generate some really long addresses (URLs). Here are some tips that might help.

- **Bookmark the page** using your browser's bookmark or favorites tools, or use a social bookmarking services such as Delicious or Diigo.

- Use a utility such as **TinyURL** (http://tinyurl.com) or **SnipURL** (http://snipurl.com) to shorten the address. Then provide the shortened address for your students.

- **Link to the page** from your blog, wiki, or webpage.

- **Create a desktop link** to your page:

    1. Open the desired page in your browser window.

    2. Resize the window so that you can see both the browser window and your desktop.

    3. Click the icon in front of the address and drag it to your desktop.

    4. Once the link is on your desktop, you can move it and rename it. You can also put the link into a folder or onto a jump drive!

       When you double-click the desktop link, your page will open in your browser.

Appendix III
Book Updates

Google Tools are constantly being updated. New features are added, and menus and buttons are modified on a fairly regular basis.

If you find that the instructions in this book no longer match the new version of a Google tool, try one or more of these options:

- Explore the screen. Many times the menus or tools have just been renamed, or they've been moved to a different location.

- Use the Help menu to find out how to complete your task.

- Challenge your students to assist in your troubleshooting.

- Perform a Google Search to find instructions and work-around tips.

Tammy will post updated screen shots and instructions on a regular basis. To view these online updates, go to:

http://googlebookupdates.tammyworcester.com